THE BEST INTERESTS
OF THE CHILD

Interpreting Irish Child Legislation

Second Edition

THE BEST INTERESTS OF THE CHILD

Interpreting Irish Child Legislation

Second Edition

Eileen McPartland

Gill & Macmillan

Gill & Macmillan
Hume Avenue
Park West
Dublin 12
www.gillmacmillan.ie

© Eileen McPartland 2013

978 07171 5719 8

Index compiled by Cliff Murphy
Print origination in Ireland by Carole Lynch
Printed in Ireland by SPRINT-print Ltd.

The paper used in this book is made from the
wood pulp of managed forests. For every tree felled,
at least one tree is planted, thereby
renewing natural resources.

A CIP catalogue record for this book is available
from the British Library.

CONTENTS

ACKNOWLEDGMENTS

For Nelser and Jemser who instilled it; Seamus who overcame and encouraged it; Aoife and Calum who have learned what it really means; Michael King who kindly reviewed the first edition; the staff and students of Liberties College who supported it; Kareen who won't be surprised; Marion, Catherine, Julia and the team at Gill & Macmillan who made it happen.

This book is dedicated with thanks to you all.

INTRODUCTION

A care contract exists in relation to children in Ireland: the team of people who look after a child in any setting must ensure that the child's best interests are paramount in caring for the child. This principle is enshrined in Irish law.

If you work with children in Ireland you are legally required to understand the relevant legislation and to keep abreast of changes in that legislation.

This book introduces the principles of law in relation to childcare and will help you understand how the law affects the care and protection of the children you look after. It is intended as an aid to learning and no legal inference should be taken from its contents.

The book opens with chapters on the Irish Constitution and the United Nations Convention on the Rights of the Child. These documents are reflected in legislation in relation to the protection and care of children in Ireland and the book highlights their influence.

The book then examines the main pieces of Irish legislation that have an impact on children's lives on a daily basis. It is essential that you know and keep up to date with such legislation.

A glossary provides explanations of terms used in the book.

CHAPTER 1

THE IRISH CONSTITUTION

One of the fundamental tools of the legislative system in Ireland is the Irish Constitution *(Bunreacht na hÉireann)*. Among other things the Constitution sets out the systems and structures of government, the law and the courts and outlines the rights of citizens. The Constitution can only be amended if a majority of the people of Ireland agree to change it in a referendum.

All laws enacted in Ireland must uphold the values and rights set out in the Constitution. To ensure that they do, all Acts pass through both Houses of the Oireachtas (the Dáil and the Seanad) before they are signed into law by the President *(Uachtarán na hÉireann)*. In some cases the President may first refer the Act to the Supreme Court or to the Council of State (a group formed under Article 31 of the Constitution) for a decision on whether it upholds the fundamental rights outlined in the Constitution.

The Constitution is divided into articles, most of which have paragraphs and sub-paragraphs. Thus, Article 1.1.1° means Article 1, paragraph 1, sub-paragraph 1 and Article 22.2.3° is Article 22, paragraph 2, sub-paragraph 3.

If you would like to view the full text of the Constitution you may download it from www. constitution.ie or purchase a copy from the Government Publications Office or other book-shops.

The current version of the Constitution mentions children under the sections relating to the family (Article 41) and to education (Article 42).

The Family

Article 41 states:

1   1° The State recognises the Family as the natural primary and fundamental unit group of Society, and as a moral institution possessing inalienable and imprescriptible rights, antecedent and superior to all positive law.

        2° The State, therefore, guarantees to protect the Family in its constitution and authority, as the necessary basis of social order and as indispensable to the welfare of the Nation and the State.

2   1° In particular, the State recognises that by her life within the home, woman gives to the State a support without which the common good cannot be achieved.

        2° The State shall, therefore, endeavour to ensure that mothers shall not be obliged by economic necessity to engage in labour to the neglect of their duties in the home.

3   1° The State pledges itself to guard with special care the institution of Marriage, on which the Family is founded, and to protect it against attack.

2° A Court designated by law may grant a dissolution of marriage where, but only where, it is satisfied that –

i   at the date of the institution of the proceedings, the spouses have lived apart from one another for a period of, or periods amounting to, at least four years during the five years,

ii   there is no reasonable prospect of a reconciliation between the spouses,

iii such provision as the Court considers proper having regard to the circumstances exists or will be made for the spouses, any children of either or both of them and any other person prescribed by law, and

iv   any further conditions prescribed by law are complied with.

3° No person whose marriage has been dissolved under the civil law of any other State but is a subsisting valid marriage under the law for the time being in force within the jurisdiction of the Government and Parliament established by this

Constitution shall be capable of contracting a valid marriage within that jurisdiction during the lifetime of the other party to the marriage so dissolved.

Article 41 has been the cause of much controversy in recent times as it recognises the 'family' and gives this 'family' significant rights. However it only recognises the family that is based on marriage. Twenty-first-century Ireland has many different types of family that are not all based on marriage and it is felt that the protections afforded in Article 41 are therefore limited in their application to some current family types.

In November 2012 the Irish people, in good faith, passed the Thirty-First Amendment of the Constitution (Children) Bill 2012 which was intended, among other things, to confer individual rights on children in Ireland. Normally this would have meant an immediate alteration to our Constitution to incorporate the changes brought about by the Referendum. However this particular Amendment has been mired in controversy, with the effect of putting it on hold until the Supreme Court hands down a written judgment regarding its finding that public money was used in such a way as to elicit a Yes vote. At the moment a challenge to its implementation has been made on the basis that the Yes vote was unfairly obtained from the people.

This new proposal might well have made a considerable difference to the notion that children's rights were only protected in the family and that the State would guarantee the protection of such rights. Currently, when cases in relation to children are brought to court, children are represented in court by their family until they reach the age of eighteen and gain their rights as an adult.

One of the relevant points in this scenario is that while there is usually a three-year limit within which a person can take a civil case against another for some harm done, the situation is a little different in the case of a child. In practice the family can take a case in such situations within three years of the wrong done to the child, but where the family does not take such a case, the child can do so within three years of reaching the age of majority (eighteen). In other words, the child has until the age of twenty-one to take a case. This limit may be extended to an even older age in extenuating circumstances, perhaps based on capacity to take a case or indeed the level of knowledge of the harm done. This point has been the subject of Supreme Court cases and it is not intended to go into the complicated details of these in this book.

Education

Until such time as a decision has been finalised on the implementation of the Thirty-First Amendment of the Constitution (Children) Referendum 2012 (currently on hold), Article 42 of the Constitution states:

1   The State acknowledges that the primary and natural educator of the child is the Family and guarantees to respect the

inalienable right and duty of parents to provide, according to their means, for the religious and moral, intellectual, physical and social education of their children.

2   Parents shall be free to provide this education in their homes or in private schools or in schools recognised or established by the State.

3   1° The State shall not oblige parents in violation of their conscience and lawful preference to send their children to schools established by the State, or to any particular type of school designated by the State.

2° The State shall, however, as guardian of the common good, require in view of actual conditions that the children receive a certain minimum education, moral, intellectual and social.

4   The State shall provide for free primary education and shall endeavour to supplement and give reasonable aid to private and corporate educational initiative, and, when the public good requires it, provide other educational facilities or institutions with due regard, however, for the rights of parents, especially in the matter of religious and moral formation.

5   In exceptional cases, where the parents for physical or moral reasons fail in their duty

towards their children, the State as guardian of the common good, by appropriate means shall endeavour to supply the place of the parents, but always with due regard for the natural and imprescriptible rights of the child.

Therefore as currently stated this article mentions the 'natural and imprescriptible rights of the child' and refers to the 'duty' of parents towards their children. However, there is no discussion of what exactly the rights of a child are or what constitutes a parent's duty. Such anomalies exist in many legal documents, which are often left open for interpretation by the courts. While some may see the lack of detail in relation to the rights of the child as a problem, others consider it a strength because when you state specific rights you limit those rights to what is stated. In the Constitution this limit does not exist and so the protection of children is all-encompassing.

The Referendum passed by the people in November 2012 removed the old paragraph 5 of Article 42 and proposed the insertion of a new Article to be known as Article 42A, which states:

1   The State recognises and affirms the natural and imprescriptible rights of all children and shall, as far as practicable, by its laws protect and vindicate those rights.

2 1° In exceptional cases, where the parents, regardless of their marital status, fail in their duty towards their children to such extent that the safety or welfare of any of their children is likely to be prejudicially affected, the State as guardian of the common good shall, by proportionate means as provided by law, endeavour to supply the place of the parents, but always with due regard for the natural and imprescriptible rights of the child.

2° Provision shall be made by law for the adoption of any child where the parents have failed for such a period of time as may be prescribed by law in their duty towards the child and where the best interests of the child so require.

3 Provision shall be made by law for the voluntary placement for adoption and the adoption of any child.

4 1° Provision shall be made by law that in the resolution of all proceedings –

    i brought by the State, as guardian of the common good, for the purpose of preventing the safety and welfare of any child from being prejudicially affected, or ii concerning the adoption, guardianship or custody of, or access to, any child, the best interests of the child shall be the paramount consideration.

2° Provision shall be made by law for securing, as far as practicable, that in all proceedings referred to in subsection 1° of this section in respect of any child who is capable of forming his or her own views, the views of the child shall be ascertained and given due weight having regard to the age and maturity of the child.

The new Article 42A (currently on hold) is a new departure in several ways. Notably section 1 does not state that the rights being conferred on the child are 'inalienable' as used in Article 41 about the rights of the family. 'Inalienable' means that they cannot be removed, transferred or altered and this is a significant consideration for future developments.

Additionally Article 42A states that the State shall 'as far as practicable by its laws protect and vindicate those rights'. This is not the same as the wording used in Article 41, where the State 'guarantees to protect'. The use of the word practicable in Article 42A allows for limitations to be placed on the protection offered, as the word 'practicable' is effectively interpreted as allowing for cost, practical or other considerations to be considered in whether it is reasonable to imple-ment the changes asked for.

The Article does however continue to state that the rights being conferred are 'imprescriptible' and the phrase 'imprescriptible rights' refers to rights that cannot be removed just because you ignore or do not use them. In other words, whether you choose to use them daily, occasionally or never choose to exercise them, these rights cannot be taken away from you.

Article 42A also introduces the notion that children can be voluntarily considered for or given up for adoption by their parents, which has not existed in Ireland before. This applies to parents 'regardless of their marital status', that is, it offers this possibility to each and every parent. This could significantly change the number of children in foster situations in Ireland, as the permission of both parents for adoption has often not been possible and children were left in a fostering limbo. This will no longer be necessary if Article 42A is eventually adopted, as agreed at referendum.

Another perhaps more fundamental change brought about by the new Article 42A is the possibility of children being taken from parents who fail to provide for them within a specific time period set by law (which would be open to change by changing the law), in which case the children (not just 'child') can be adopted to protect their best interests. The possibility exists that, where a parent is given a custodial sentence longer than this time period set by law, then the child could be adopted while the parent is in jail. There are other reasons why parents may not provide for their children, and in many cases the notion that adoption is an option offers some children better outcomes than they currently have.

Another development in Article 42A is the concept that in proceedings brought by the state concerning the changes referred to in Article 42A, the best interests of the child shall be paramount and that the views of the child must be 'ascertained and given due weight having regard to the age and maturity of the child'. The views of the child are however not guaranteed to result in any changes but must merely be listened to.

Fundamental to any discussion on the new Article 42A is the concept that rights protected by laws are not the same as rights protected in the Constitution, as the law can be changed by politicians while the Constitution can only be changed by the agreement of the people at referendum.

CHAPTER 2

UN CONVENTION ON THE RIGHTS OF THE CHILD

In 1989 world leaders got together to draw up a legally binding agreement to protect children, recognising that children are a vulnerable part of society. The result was the United Nations (UN) Convention on the Rights of the Child, which sets out those rights in fifty-four articles and two optional protocols. The text of the Convention is reproduced in Appendix 3 of this book.

The Convention is not a piece of legislation in itself but it has shaped laws that have been passed since 1989 in Ireland and in other countries in relation to the care and welfare of children. Conventions are ratified (accepted and agreed to) by countries who accept their basic principles and agree to incorporate their ideals into the laws of that country.

In essence the Convention on the Rights of the Child states that children have basic human rights: to survival; to develop to their fullest potential; to protection from harmful influences, abuse and exploitation; and to participate fully in family, cultural and social life. This chapter highlights some of the key sections of the Convention.

Core Principles

The four core principles of the Convention are:

- Non-discrimination
- Devotion to the best interests of the child
- The right to life, survival and development
- Respect for the views of the child.

It is important to remember these core principles when looking at legislation that has been passed in countries that have ratified the Convention. Such countries have committed to these principles and you will see these expressions used in their laws.

Ireland has incorporated many aspects of the Convention into its laws and the four core principles are evident in the words and ideals of Irish legislation in relation to children. One of the main Acts passed in Ireland since ratifying the Convention is the Child Care Act 1991, which has clearly adopted these core values and the above expressions can be found in its text.

Preamble

The Preamble reminds us that the United Nations stated in the Universal Declaration of Human Rights that 'childhood is entitled to special care and assistance' and also recognises the family 'as the fundamental group of society' (just as the Irish Constitution did in 1937). It stresses the ideal that children should be cared for and protected until they are in a position to lead an 'individual life in society'. Not surprisingly, the ideals of the Convention on the Rights of the Child sit easily alongside Irish laws.

Article 1

Article 1 sets out the definition of a child as someone under the age of eighteen unless otherwise defined in the laws of an individual country.

In the case of Ireland, the Disability Act 2005 sets the age at eighteen, as does the Child Care Act 1991. The Disability Act 2005 goes further by saying that a person with a disability of such an extent that the person cannot live an independent life without support is entitled to the protections of a child under the Act. The Act defines a disability as follows:

> 'Disability', in relation to a person, means a substantial restriction in the capacity of the person to carry on a profession, business or occupation in the State or to participate in social or cultural life in the State by reason of an enduring physical, sensory, mental health or intellectual impairment.

The Act explains the term 'substantial restriction' in relation to a disability as:

> (a) is permanent or likely to be permanent, results in a significant difficulty in communication, learning or mobility or in significantly disordered cognitive processes, and

(b)   gives rise to the need for services to be provided continually to the person whether or not a child or, if the person is a child, to the need for services to be provided early in life to ameliorate the disability.

The age at which a person is no longer a child in relation to the legal system is eighteen in Ireland, except in the case of disability where it could be older than eighteen. It is not a clear cut-off at eighteen and as a person working with children you need to ensure that you apply this distinction. You cannot assume that the person in front of you has the capacity to understand the implications of some decisions you may require that person to make. Depending on the capacity of the person in the situation you may need to seek the agreement of parents or people *in loco parentis* (in the place of parents) for some issues that may arise, even though the person is over eighteen years old.

Article 2

Article 2 seeks to protect children from discrim-ination on grounds similar to the nine grounds now stated under Ireland's Equal Status Acts 2000 to 2004. It specifically states that children should not be discriminated against or punished on the basis of the actions, beliefs or stated opinions of their parents, legal guardians or family members. This article has the potential to have far-reaching implications.

Article 3

Every person working with children should note this article. It is one of the most fundamental aspects of the Convention as it states that the primary consideration in relation to a child will be 'the best interests of the child'. This is the most important aspect of good practice in relation to the care of children in Ireland, and the Child Care Act 1991 and subsequent Acts are all concerned with promoting 'the best interests of the child'.

Article 3 also states that children should be cared for by competent people, in suitable situations that meet set supervisory standards. This has relevance to the process of National Vetting in Ireland for people working with children. The suitability of staff, institutions, services and facilities are the duty of states parties that have adopted the Convention and this includes suitability and competence in relation to training and understanding the needs of the children in your care.

The fundamentals of Irish rules for childcare facilities are set out in the childcare regulations (the most recent being the Child Care (Pre-School Services) (No. 2) Regulations 2006, which came into effect on 1 September 2007). The regulations set out such things as the minimum carer/child ratios and space provisions required for any pre-school facility in Ireland. These limits ensure that the child's safety and welfare are taken into account. In relation to other care situations, stipulations in various relevant Acts describe 'recognised' or 'approved' centres that are overseen by the state, which is charged with the duty to ensure the suitability of such establishments under this article of the Convention.

The protection of the best interests of the child is a fundamental undertaking of any childcare worker and the inclusion of this expression in Article 42A, (if finalised), will ensure its incorporation into the Constitution. However the expression on its own does not provide an explanation of what is involved in the concept and in many cases the best interests of the child are open to interpretation by adults who legislate on behalf of children, whether in the role of parent or *in loco parentis* (in the place of parents).

Article 5

This article states that parents have 'rights and duties' and it extends these duties to people who are in the place of parents (*in loco parentis*) for whatever reason. As with the Irish Constitution, the concepts of rights and duties are mentioned together in this article. The duty appears to be owed to the child in the case of the Convention. The Convention recognises that these rights and duties will change over time depending on 'the evolving capacities of the child'.

Articles 9, 19 and 25

Article 9 goes a little further in relation to the concept that a duty is owed to a child. It states that children should receive assistance from the state to contact their parent(s) when they have been separated – this might mean in different countries and other certain circumstances – *except* where it is not in 'the best interests of the child' to do so.

This principle has been incorporated into the Protection of Children (Hague Convention) Act 2000, which deals with issues such as the concept of jurisdiction, enforcement of parental rights, co-operation in relation to the protection of children and repatriation of children who have been abducted. The Act allows for orders to be made by a District Court judge in relation to a parent seeking access to his or her child. In this aim the District Court judge may exercise the jurisdiction of either the District or Circuit Court in emergency situations to decide in the best interests of the child if one parent qualifies for access.

Article 19 endorses the use of educational measures (such as parenting or counselling courses) to protect the child from abuse, negligence, maltreatment or exploitation while in the care of parents or others *in loco parentis*. Such measures would also include social programmes of support for the child and those charged with the child's care. This stance is based on the conviction stated in the Preamble that 'the family, as the fundamental group of society and the natural environment for the growth and well-being of all its members and particularly children, should be afforded the necessary protection and assistance so that it can fully assume its responsibilities within the community'.

Article 25 recognises the right of a child in the care of a competent authority to have that care provision reviewed periodically. This right will be discussed further when we examine the Mental Health Act 2001.

These articles form the basis of Ireland's child protection provisions in the Child Care Act 1991, where the goal is clearly stated as being the best interests of the child. To this end the protection of the child is stated as being in a family situation except in cases where to do so is not in the child's best interests.

Article 12

Article 12 gives children the right to form their own opinions and views and to express them. This right has been evident in Ireland in the selection process for the post of Ombudsman for Children, which involved children in choosing the best candidate for the job. Indeed the ongoing work of the Ombudsman's Office continues to invite the opinions of children in relation to their lives and experiences.

The article goes even further by stating that a child has a right to representation in judicial or administrative proceedings in relation to that child. Ireland has sought to include these ideals in legislation, specifically in the Child Care Act 1991.

Article 42A, if finally inserted into the Constitution, will also state that in relation to adoption cases, whether voluntary or where parents have failed to adequately provide for their children for a specified time, the opinions of the child in the case should be listened to. This is in line with Article 12 of the Convention on the Rights of the Child, except that Article 42A allows for 'due weight' to be given to the age and stage of development of the child – somewhat a dilution of the idea that a child will have a full say or even be guaranteed that their wishes will be applied.

Article 23

This article deals with children with disabilities and their right to inclusion, full participation and effective access to and participation 'in a manner conducive to the child's achieving the fullest possible social integration and individual development, including his or her cultural and spiritual development'. This goal underpins Ireland's Education for Persons with Special Educational Needs Act 2004 and Disability Act 2005.

Article 28

Article 28 forms the basis of Ireland's Education (Welfare) Act 2000 from the point of view of putting in place measures to ensure school attendance and the need to reduce drop-out rates.

Article 31

Article 31 sets out the rights of children to play, recreation, artistic expression and participation in culture. Every person who works with children must ensure that the rights of children are adhered to within their work and this right to play, recreation and artistic expression as well as participation in culture can direct some of the work done with children. Every crèche, school, playgroup and other child-centred facility must ensure that these elements are covered in its daily routines as children often spend as much time there as they do with their parents in modern society.

The on-hold Article 42A in some ways goes towards ensuring Ireland lives up to the promises it made in ratifying the United Nations Convention on the Rights of the Child and it will be interesting to see what interpretations will be effected after the legislature (specifically the courts) start to interpret its provisions.

CHAPTER 3

CHILD CARE ACT 1991

The Child Care Act 1991 is very important in relation to the protection of children. It was enacted after the UN Convention on the Rights of the Child and the ideals of the Convention can be recognised in the wording of the Act, including use of the expression 'the best interests of the child'. The Act puts a legal responsibility on any person charged with the care of any child to act in the child's best interests – this is the most fundamental requirement of every person who works with children in whatever situation.

The Act defines a child as a person under the age of eighteen, except someone who is or has been married (this has been modified since, as already explained in the discussion above on the Disability Act 2005).

The Act is divided into ten parts, some of which are administrative. This chapter outlines the key parts of the Act, which any person working in childcare or any student of childcare must know and understand.

Part II

This part charges the health boards (now the Health Service Executive) with the welfare of children in their region and provides for the establishment of childcare advisory committees in each health service area.

Part III

Part III allows for gardaí to remove a child from a situation of immediate danger and to make an emergency care order in relation to that child. It recognises that the best place for a child is with the family, as provided for in the Constitution and indeed in the Convention on the Rights of the Child, but acknowledges that sometimes a child is in immediate danger with the family and must be taken elsewhere.

Part IV

This part underlines Ireland's commitment to the principles of the Convention on the Rights of the Child in so far as there is a legal requirement to go to court to review emergency care orders. It also allows for interim care orders, care orders and supervision orders with judicial review of decisions made on behalf of the child in question.

Part V

Part V allows for a child to receive legal representation in relation to the orders by allowing for the appointment by the court of a solicitor and guardian *ad litem* (who represents the best interests of the child) and also provides that the privacy of the child be protected and the child's welfare prioritised.

Part VI

Children can be placed in foster care or residential care or some family care that is in their best interests. This part also provides for periodic reviews and supervision as outlined in the Convention on the Rights of the Child.

Part VII

Part VII relates to what childcare workers need to know in order to do their job properly, thus fulfilling the requirement in the Convention on the Rights of the Child that the child be cared for in a competent institution.

This part also provides for childcare regulations to underpin the operation of childcare facilities, including stating the space requirements for every child in a setting and the carer/child ratios. It is important to note that the actual regulations are not contained in the Child Care Act 1991, thus avoiding the need to amend the whole Act every time a change is made to the regulations. The regulations are separate and are updated from time to time to take account of changes in policy in relation to the operation of child-centred facilities.

Part VIII

This part provides for the registration, staffing, services and facilities of residential centres.

———

There is no doubt that the Childcare Act 1991 is dated, particularly in relation to the changes envisioned if Article 42A is to come into effect. It was proposed to amend this Act under the Children First 2012 Bill, which has also been put on hold pending a final decision on Article 42A. Specifically there would be changes to the idea that just the best interests of the child be taken into account, as any new provisions would also have to ensure that a correct procedure for the establishment of the child's view, and its interpretation, be included in any new laws.

Despite the introduction of the Child Care Act 1991, which is the definitive Act in relation to child protection in Ireland, people remained reluctant, for fear of repercussions, to make a report of abuse that might result in a child being removed from a family. This reluctance limited the effectiveness of the Act and necessitated the passing of further legislation, namely the Protection for Persons Reporting Child Abuse Act 1998.

CHAPTER 4

PROTECTION FOR PERSONS REPORTING CHILD ABUSE ACT 1998

The Protection for Persons Reporting Child Abuse Act 1998 provides immunity from being sued for damages for people who report suspicions of abuse 'reasonably and in good faith' to designated health service staff or to gardaí. It also protects employees from being sacked from employment or being discriminated against because they may have made a report of child abuse 'reasonably and in good faith'. This Act is fundamental to the effectiveness of the Child Care Act 1991 as, prior to its passing, people were afraid of being sued when they reported a suspicion of child abuse.

The Act states that a suspicion of abuse consists of an opinion that:

(a)   a child has been or is being assaulted, ill-treated, neglected or sexually abused, or

(b)   a child's health, development or welfare has been or is being avoidably impaired or neglected

The Act has no protection for somebody who makes a false allegation 'knowing' the statement made to be 'false'; indeed it provides for prosecution on criminal charges in such cases. This measure protects people from malicious acts in relation to child abuse reporting.

Importantly the Act does not require mandatory reporting of suspicions of abuse, its aim is just to protect those who do report their suspicions. It does not protect a person who reports a suspicion from threats and intimidation in their everyday life, however, and this may be a failing in the Act as in some societal situations intimidation is a part of everyday life for people.

The provisions of *Children First: National Guidance for the Protection and Welfare of Children* (2011) make it clear that every person, whether a professional or not, must consider the welfare of the child as paramount in cases where abuse is suspected. This effectively says that the person's own protection should not be the deciding factor in whether or not to report suspected abuse of children.

Role of Childcare Worker

Children First: National Guidance for the Protection and Welfare of Children (2011) sets out detailed procedures to be followed by organisations in relation to child protection as well as defining the different forms of abuse in concise terms (see Chapter 5). Every worker, or student, working with children should be familiar with these definitions as part of their work skills.

The guidance requires you to be vigilant in your work and to make a note of things that you observe in relation to the children in your care. The observation methods you learn as a student will be the ones you use in relation to child protection and you should be confident that the observations you make can be used as part of a body of evidence in a child protection situation, should that prove necessary.

To this end the importance of keeping a reflective diary in relation to working in any setting that involves the care and support of children cannot be overstated. Only by reflection can you put in context what you see and how you carry out your work with children. It is a process that changes continually as the child develops within your care and contemporaneous notes (those made as you go along) can form the basis of a child's protection where things are not correct.

Always remember:

Working in childcare is a team effort and all members work together in the best interests of the child

Anybody working with children should be proud to be part of the care contract which ensures that the child's best interests are met. The care contract requires you to always consider how your actions impact on the child in your care and how best that impact should be directed to ensure that the child gets the most out of your interaction together, bearing in mind the child's age, stage of development and evolving capacities.

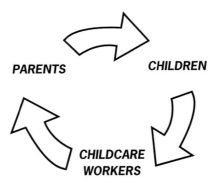

While observation is hugely important in this process, discipline, professionalism, insight, trust, mutual respect and consideration and the ability to predict the needs of a child in any given situation are also fundamental concepts in your working relationship with children.

CHAPTER 5

DEFINITIONS OF ABUSE

This chapter sets out the exact definitions of abuse as given in *Children First: National Guidance for the Protection and Welfare of Children* (2011) (Chapters 2 and 3). Appendix 8 of the guidance requires that where definitions of abuse are used they are specifically as outlined in Chapters 2 and 3 of the guidance and are not to be changed or adapted. This is stated as being for the purpose of ensuring that there is consistency on definitions, the basis for reporting and the standard reporting procedure.

Definitions of Child Abuse

This section outlines the principal types of child abuse and offers guidance on how to recognise such abuse. Child abuse can be categorised into four different types: neglect, emotional abuse, physical abuse and sexual abuse. A child may be subjected to one or more forms of abuse at any given time. More detail on each type of abuse is given in Appendix 1 of this book.

In the guidance, a 'child' means a person under the age of 18 years, excluding a person who is or has been married.

Definition of 'Neglect'

Neglect can be defined in terms of an omission, where the child suffers significant harm or impairment of development by being deprived of food, clothing, warmth, hygiene, intellectual stimulation, supervision and safety, attachment to and affection from adults, and/or medical care.

Harm can be defined as the ill-treatment or the impairment of the health or development of a child. Whether it is significant is determined by the child's health and development as compared to that which could reasonably be expected of a child of similar age.

Neglect generally becomes apparent in different ways over a period of time rather than at one specific point. For example, a child who suffers a series of minor injuries may not be having his or her needs met in terms of necessary supervision and safety. A child whose height or weight is significantly below average may be being deprived of adequate nutrition. A child who consistently misses school may be being deprived of intellectual stimulation.

The threshold of significant harm is reached when the child's needs are neglected to the extent that his or her well-being and/or development are severely affected.

Definition of 'Emotional Abuse'

Emotional abuse is normally to be found in the relationship between a parent/carer and a child rather than in a specific event or pattern of events. It occurs when a child's developmental need for affection, approval, consistency and security are not met. Unless other forms of abuse are present, it is rarely manifested in terms of physical signs or symptoms. Examples may include:

  (i) the imposition of negative attributes on a child, expressed by persistent criticism, sarcasm, hostility or blaming;

 (ii) conditional parenting in which the level of care shown to a child is made contingent on his or her behaviours or actions;

(iii) emotional unavailability of the child's parent/carer;

 (iv) unresponsiveness of the parent/carer and/or inconsistent or inappropriate expectations of the child;

  (v) premature imposition of responsibility on the child;

 (vi) unrealistic or inappropriate expectations of the child's capacity to understand something or to behave and control himself or herself in a certain way;

(vii) under- or over-protection of the child;

(viii) failure to show interest in, or provide age-appropriate opportunities for, the child's cognitive and emotional development;

 (ix) use of unreasonable or over-harsh disciplinary measures;

  (x) exposure to domestic violence;

(xi) exposure to inappropriate or abusive material through new technology.

Emotional abuse can be manifested in terms of the child's behavioural, cognitive, affective or physical functioning. Examples of these include insecure attachment, unhappiness, low self-esteem, educational and developmental underachievement, and oppositional behaviour. The threshold of significant harm is reached when abusive interactions dominate and become typical of the relationship between the child and the parent/carer.

Definition of 'Physical Abuse'

Physical abuse of a child is that which results in actual or potential physical harm from an interaction, or lack of interaction, which is reasonably within the control of a parent or person in a position of responsibility, power or trust. There may be single or repeated incidents.

Physical abuse can involve:

(i) severe physical punishment;
(ii) beating, slapping, hitting or kicking;
(iii) pushing, shaking or throwing;
(iv) pinching, biting, choking or hair-pulling;
(v) terrorising with threats;
(vi) observing violence;
(vii) use of excessive force in handling;
(viii) deliberate poisoning;
(ix) suffocation;

(x) fabricated/induced illness (see Appendix 1 for details);

(xi) allowing or creating a substantial risk of significant harm to a child.

Definition of 'Sexual Abuse'

Sexual abuse occurs when a child is used by another person for his or her gratification or sexual arousal, or for that of others. Examples of child sexual abuse include:

(i) exposure of the sexual organs or any sexual act intentionally performed in the presence of the child;

(ii) intentional touching or molesting of the body of a child whether by a person or object for the purpose of sexual arousal or gratification;

(iii) masturbation in the presence of the child or the involvement of the child in an act of masturbation;

(iv) sexual intercourse with the child, whether oral, vaginal or anal;

(v) sexual exploitation of a child, which includes inciting, encouraging, propositioning, requiring or permitting a child to solicit for, or to engage in, prostitution or other sexual acts. Sexual exploitation also occurs when a child is involved in exhibition, modelling or posing for the purpose of sexual arousal, gratification or sexual act, including its recording (on film, video tape or other media) or the manipulation, for those purposes, of the image by computer or other means. It may also include showing sexually explicit material to children, which is often a feature of the 'grooming' process by perpetrators of abuse;

(vi) consensual sexual activity involving an adult and an underage person. In relation to child sexual abuse, it should be noted that, for the purposes of the criminal law, the age of consent to sexual intercourse is 17 years for both boys and girls. An Garda Síochána will deal with the criminal aspects of the case under the relevant legislation.

It should be noted that the definition of child sexual abuse presented in this section is not a legal definition and is not intended to be a description of the criminal offence of sexual assault.

Recognising Child Neglect or Abuse

Child neglect or abuse can often be difficult to identify and may present in many forms. A list of indicators of child abuse is contained in Appendix 1. No one indicator should be seen as conclusive in itself of abuse. It may indicate conditions other than child abuse. All signs and symptoms must be examined in the context of the child's situation and family circumstances.

Guidelines for Recognition

The ability to recognise child abuse can depend as much on a person's willingness to accept the possibility of its existence as it does on their knowledge and information. There are commonly three stages in the identification of child neglect or abuse:

Stage 1: Considering the possibility

The possibility of child abuse should be considered if a child appears to have suffered a suspicious injury for which no reasonable explanation can be offered. It should also be considered if the child seems distressed without obvious reason or displays persistent or new behavioural problems. The possibility of child abuse should also be considered if the child displays unusual or fearful responses to parents/carers or older children. A pattern of ongoing neglect should also be considered even when there are short periods of improvement.

Stage 2: Looking out for signs of neglect or abuse

Signs of neglect or abuse can be physical, behavioural or developmental. They can exist in the relationships between children and parents/carers or between children and other family members/ other persons. A cluster or pattern of signs is more likely to be indicative of neglect or abuse. Children who are being abused may hint that they are being harmed and sometimes make direct disclosures. Disclosures should always be taken very seriously and should be acted upon, for example, by informing the HSE Children and Family Services. The child should not be interviewed in detail about the alleged abuse without first consulting with the HSE Children and Family Services. This may be more appropriately carried out by a social worker or An Garda Síochána. Less obvious signs could be gently explored with the child, without direct questioning. Play situations, such as drawing or story-telling, may reveal information.

Some signs are more indicative of abuse than others. These include:

(i) disclosure of abuse by a child or young person;

(ii) age-inappropriate or abnormal sexual play or knowledge;

(iii) specific injuries or patterns of injuries;

(iv) absconding from home or a care situation;

(v) attempted suicide;

(vi) underage pregnancy or sexually transmitted disease;

(vii) signs in one or more categories at the same time. For example, signs of developmental delay, physical injury and behavioural signs may together indicate a pattern of abuse.

Many signs of abuse are non-specific and must be considered in the child's social and family context. It is important to be open to alternative explanations for physical or behavioural signs of abuse.

Stage 3: Recording of information

If neglect or abuse is suspected and acted upon, for example, by informing the HSE Children and Family Services, it is important to establish the grounds for concern by obtaining as much information as possible. Observations should be accurately recorded and should include dates, times, names, locations, context and any other information that may be relevant. Care should be taken as to how such information is stored and to whom it is made available.

Children with Additional Vulnerabilities

Certain children are more vulnerable to abuse than others. Such children include those with disabilities, children who are homeless and those who, for one reason or another, are separated from their parents or other family members and who depend on others for their care and protection. The same categories of abuse – neglect, emotional abuse, physical abuse and sexual abuse – are applicable, but may take a slightly different form. For example, abuse may take the form of deprivation of basic rights, harsh disciplinary regimes or the inappropriate use of medications or physical restraints (see also Chapter 8 of *Children First: National Guidance for the Protection and Welfare of Children* (2011)).

Fatal Child Abuse

In the tragic circumstances where a child dies as a result of abuse or neglect, there are four important aspects to be considered: criminal, child protection, bereavement and notification.

Criminal aspects: These are the responsibility of An Garda Síochána and they must be notified immediately. The Coroner must also be notified and his or her instructions complied with in relation to post-mortems and other relevant matters.

Child protection aspects: These will be particularly relevant if there are other children in the family or in the same situation, and will therefore require immediate intervention by the HSE Children and Family Services to assess risk.

Bereavement aspects: The bereavement needs of the family must be respected and provided for and all family members should be given an opportunity to grieve and say goodbye to the deceased child.

Notification aspects: The HSE should notify the death of a child to the National Review Panel and to the Health Information and Quality Authority in accordance with the HIQA's *Guidance for the Health Service Executive for the Review of Serious Incidents, including deaths of children in care* (HIQA, 2010):

- all deaths of children in care, including natural causes;
- all deaths of children known to the child protection system;

- serious incidents involving a child in care or known to the child protection services.

Managers and staff should co-operate fully with any review undertaken to establish the facts of the case and any actions that should be taken, to identify learning that will improve services in the future and to provide assurance to the public.

Points to Remember

The severity of a sign does not necessarily equate with the severity of the abuse. Severe and potentially fatal injuries are not always visible. Neglect and emotional and/or psychological abuse tend to be cumulative and effects may only be observable in the longer term. Explanations that are inconsistent with the signs should constitute a cause for concern.

Neglect is as potentially fatal as physical abuse. It can cause delayed physical, psychological and emotional development, chronic ill-health and significant long-term damage. It may place children at serious risk of harm. It may also precede or co-exist with other forms of abuse and must be acted upon.

Experiencing recurring low-level abuse may cause serious and long-term harm. Cumulative harm refers to the effects of multiple adverse circumstances and events in a child's life. The unremitting daily impact of these circumstances on the child can be profound and exponential, and diminish a child's sense of safety and well-being.

Child abuse is not restricted to any socio-economic group, gender or culture. All signs must be considered in the wider social and family context. Serious deficits in child safety and welfare transcend cultural, social and ethnic norms, and must elicit a response.

Challenging behaviour by a child or young person should not render them liable to abuse. Children in certain circumstances may present management problems. This should not leave them vulnerable to harsh disciplinary measures or neglect of care.

Exposure to domestic violence is detrimental to children's physical, emotional and psychological well-being. The adverse effects of domestic violence have been well established.

While the impact of neglect is most profound on young children, it also adversely affects adolescents. Neglect renders young people liable to risk-taking behaviours, such as running away, early school-leaving, anti-social behaviour, mental health and addiction problems, including the risk of suicide.

It is sometimes difficult to distinguish between indicators of child abuse and other adversities suffered by children and families. Deprivation, stress, addiction or mental health problems should not be used as a justification for omissions of care or commissions of harm by parents/carers. The child's welfare must be the primary consideration.

Neglectful families may be difficult to engage. Research shows that families may be reluctant to seek help in response to experiencing the factors associated with neglect.

Families where neglect and abuse are prevalent may go to considerable lengths to deceive professionals. It is important for professionals to approach cases with a wary trustfulness, seek evidence to substantiate claims of improvement and speak with the children concerned individually.

Social workers need good observation and analytical skills in order to be able to understand the nature of the relationship between a parent and child, to understand signs of non-compliance, to work alongside a family and to come to safe and evidence-based judgments about the best course of action.

Working in the area of child abuse and neglect is dealing with uncertainty. Social workers and other professionals should adopt a 'respectful uncertainty' on parental reporting of improvement until supported by clear evidence.

Role of Childcare Worker

There is no doubt that, in the construction of these definitions, regard was given to the many reports into child abuse carried out in Ireland in the recent past. To understand why these specific definitions are necessary one need only read some of the following reports:

- The Ryan Report
- The Dublin Archdiocese Report

- The Ferns Report
- The Cloyne Report
- The Kilkenny Report
- The Roscommon Report
- The TF Report
- The Report of the Independent Child Death Review Group

They make harrowing reflections on past systems of child protection in Ireland and should inform our best practices in the future.

As a childcare worker you need to be aware that the above signs and symptoms may not occur on a one-off basis and usually there is a pattern of behaviour that alerts you to suspect child abuse – reasonableness and proper observation play a huge part in such situations. In this respect the precise recording of observations and the keeping of a reflective diary are essential to the proper care and observation of children in your care.

It is important to note that physical signs may not be evident in cases of sexual abuse due to the nature of the abuse and/or the fact that the disclosure was made some time after the abuse took place.

Where you notice significant changes in a child's behaviour you should be prompted to question why this is so and what you can do to rectify the situation. You should familiarise yourself with the procedures to follow in the facility you are working in and ensure that you follow them correctly where abuse is suspected. Remember also that not every suspicion will be founded and you need to take an objective view of what you see. There may be situations where, for example, a younger child is unable to articulate a worry and in such circumstances your listening to what the child is actually saying may be a relief to that child and alter the behaviour you thought was out of the ordinary.

Your constant focus must be on the best interests of the child and more specifically the best interests of the actual child in front of you whose individual needs will change with his or her level of knowledge, understanding and development, or in the words of the UN Convention on the Rights of the Child with his or her 'evolving capacities'.

You also should ensure that you do not unwittingly put yourself in situations where you might be open to an accusation of abuse. In this regard you should at all times follow the policies and procedures that are set out for your workplace – they are there to protect everybody.

The significance of protecting yourself should also be borne in mind in relation to the passing into law of the recent National Vetting Bureau (Children and Vulnerable Persons) Act 2012 which will apply to anybody who works in childcare or with vulnerable persons. This Act allows the new National Vetting Bureau to replace the Garda Vetting Bureau and to exchange information from the Garda database in relation to what is called 'soft' information about a person. This refers to information that does not amount to criminal conviction but may include suspicions that existed but were held not to be substantiated. If nothing else this Act should waken every childcare worker to the possibility that if they do not carefully follow the policies and procedures of the setting they may well unwittingly affect their future job potential.

While it would be expected that such information may not reasonably have been disclosed to the Gardaí, the Act provides for Compliance Officers who can enter the premises of an organisation and inspect its records and books, and thus collect such soft information.

CHAPTER 6

REPORTING CHILD ABUSE

The following is taken from *Children First: National Guidance for the Protection and Welfare of Children* (2011) as required by Appendix 8 of that document.

This section offers guidance to the general public and to all people, both professional and voluntary, working with or in direct contact with children, who may be concerned or who suspect that children are being abused or neglected or are at risk of abuse or neglect. It outlines the standard reporting procedure to be used in passing information to the statutory authorities about child protection concerns.

Responsibility to Report Child Abuse or Neglect

Everyone must be alert to the possibility that children with whom they are in contact may be suffering from abuse or neglect. This responsibility is particularly relevant for professionals such as teachers, childcare workers, health professionals and those working with adults with serious parenting difficulties. It is also an important responsibility for staff and people involved in sports clubs, community activities, youth clubs, the religious/faith sector and other organisations catering for children.

The HSE Children and Family Services should always be informed when a person has reasonable grounds for concern that a child may have been, is being or is at risk of being abused or neglected.

Child protection concerns should be supported by evidence that indicates the possibility of abuse or neglect.

A concern about a potential risk to children posed by a specific person, even if the children are unidentifiable, should also be communicated to the HSE Children and Family Services.

The guiding principles in regard to reporting child abuse or neglect may be summarised as follows:

   (i) the safety and well-being of the child must take priority;

  (ii) reports should be made without delay to the HSE Children and Family Services.

Any reasonable concern or suspicion of abuse or neglect must elicit a response. Ignoring the signals or failing to intervene may result in ongoing or further harm to the child.

Section 176 of the Criminal Justice Act 2006 introduced the criminal charge of reckless endangerment of children. It states:

> A person, having authority or control over a child or abuser, who intentionally or recklessly endangers a child by –
>
>   (a) causing or permitting any child to be placed or left in a situation which

> creates a substantial risk to the child of being a victim of serious harm or sexual abuse, or
>
> (b)   failing to take reasonable steps to protect a child from such a risk while knowing that the child is in such a situation, is guilty of an offence.

The penalty for a person found guilty of this offence is a fine (no upper limit) and/or imprisonment for a term not exceeding ten years.

The HSE has a statutory obligation to identify children who are not receiving adequate care and protection, to provide family support services and, where necessary, to take children into the care of the HSE. People who report concerns need to be assured that their information will be carefully considered with any other information available, and a child protection assessment will only proceed where sufficient risk is identified.

Any professional who suspects child abuse or neglect should inform the parents/carers if a report is to be submitted to the HSE Children and Family Services or to An Garda Síochána, unless doing so is likely to endanger the child.

The HSE will respect, as much as possible, the wishes of non-professionals reporting concerns in good faith who ask to remain anonymous, but cannot give a guarantee that the information would not be sought and given within judicial proceedings. (The Data Protection Acts offer protection under privacy, but should the information be sought directly within legal proceedings, there is no guarantee.)

Designated Liaison Persons for Reporting Neglect or Abuse

Every organisation, both public and private, that is providing services for children or that is in regular direct contact with children should:

(i) Identify a designated liaison person to act as a liaison with outside agencies and a resource person for any staff member or volunteer who has child protection concerns.

(ii) The designated liaison person is responsible for ensuring that the standard reporting procedure is followed, so that suspected cases of child neglect or abuse are referred promptly to the designated person in the HSE Children and Family Services or in the event of an emergency and the unavailability of the HSE, to An Garda Síochána.

(iii) The designated liaison person should ensure that they are knowledgeable about child protection and undertake any training considered necessary to keep themselves updated on new developments.

Standard Reporting Procedure

Any person reporting a child abuse or neglect concern should do so without delay to the HSE

Children and Family Services. A report can be made in person, by telephone or in writing. Contact numbers for all HSE offices nationwide are given in Appendix 2 of the national guidance and are also available on the HSE website (www.hse.ie) or through the HSE LoCall Tel. 1850 241850.

Before deciding whether or not to make a formal report, you may wish to discuss your concerns with a health professional or directly with the HSE Children and Family Services.

Under no circumstances should a child be left in a situation that exposes him or her to harm or to risk of harm pending HSE intervention. In the event of an emergency where you think a child is in immediate danger and you cannot get in contact with the HSE, you should contact the Gardaí. This may be done through any Garda station.

The Standard Report Form for reporting child welfare and protection concerns to the HSE (Appendix 3 of the guidance document and Appendix 2 of this book) should be used by professionals, staff and volunteers in organisations working with or in contact with children or providing services to children, when reporting child protection and welfare concerns to the HSE Children and Family Services. If a report is made by telephone, this form should be completed and forwarded subsequently to the HSE.

The HSE will follow up on all referrals, even if the Standard Report Form has not been used.

Information to Be Included When Making a Report

The ability of the HSE Children and Family Services or An Garda Síochána to assess and investigate suspicions or allegations of child abuse or neglect will depend on the amount and quality of information conveyed to them by people reporting concerns. As much as possible of the following detail should be provided:

   (i) the name, address and age of the child (or children) for whom the report is being made;

  (ii) the name of the child's school;

 (iii) the name and contact details of the person reporting concerns;

 (iv) whether the person reporting is a professional, a person working with children or a member of the public;

  (v) the relationship to the child of the person making the report;

 (vi) a full account of what constitutes the grounds for concern in relation to the protection and welfare of the child or children, e.g. details of the allegation, incident, dates, description of any injuries, etc.;

 (vii) the names and addresses of the parents/ carers of the child or children;

(viii) the names of other children in the household;

 (ix) the name, address and details of the person allegedly causing concern in relation to the child or children;

(x) the child's and/or parents'/carers' own views, if known and relevant;

(xi) the names and addresses of other personnel or agencies involved with the child or children, e.g. GP, social worker, public health nurse, Gardaí, etc.;

(xii) any other relevant information.

Retrospective Disclosures by Adults

An increasing number of adults are disclosing abuse that took place during their childhoods. Such disclosures often come to light when adults attend counselling. It is essential to establish whether there is any current risk to any child who may be in contact with the alleged abuser revealed in such disclosures.

If any risk is deemed to exist to a child who may be in contact with an alleged abuser, the counsellor or health professional should report the allegation to the HSE Children and Family Services without delay.

The HSE National Counselling Service is in place to listen to, value and understand those who have been abused in childhood. The service is a professional, confidential counselling and psychotherapy service and is available free of charge in all regions of the country (see www.hse-ncs.ie/en).

The service can be accessed either through healthcare professionals or by way of self-referral (Freephone 1800 477477).

Deciding to Share Child Protection Concerns

The belief that parents, carers or other persons in charge of children would actually harm or neglect them is not easy to sustain. There may be a tendency, therefore, to deny, minimise or explain away any signs that a child is being harmed, even when evidence exists. At times, it is hard to distinguish between abusive situations and those where other problems are present, such as unemployment, poverty, poor housing, addiction, mental illness or isolation. Sympathy for families in difficult circumstances can sometimes dilute personal or professional concerns about the safety and welfare of children. However, the protection and welfare of the child must always be the paramount concern.

Reluctance to act on suspicions about child abuse or neglect can often stem from uncertainty and fear. Members of the public or professionals may be afraid of repercussions, afraid of being thought insensitive, afraid of breaking a confidence or afraid of being disloyal. Knowledge and information about child abuse will help to overcome reluctance to take action. So too will confidence in the child protection and welfare services.

It is the responsibility of all agencies working with children and for the public to recognise child protection concerns and share these with the agencies responsible for assessing or investigating them, not to determine whether the child protection concerns are evidenced or not.

Cases Not Reported to the HSE or An Garda Síochána

In those cases where an organisation decides not to report concerns to the HSE or An Garda Síochána, the individual employee or volunteer who raised the concern should be given a clear written statement of the reasons why the organisation is not taking such action. The employee or volunteer should be advised that if they remain concerned about the situation, they are free as individuals to consult with, or report to, the HSE or An Garda Síochána. The provisions of the Protections for Persons Reporting Child Abuse Act 1998 apply once they communicate 'reasonably and in good faith'.

Confidentiality

The effective protection of a child often depends on the willingness of the staff in statutory and voluntary organisations involved with children to share and exchange relevant information. It is therefore critical that there is a clear understanding of professional and legal responsibilities with regard to confidentiality and the exchange of information.

All information regarding concern or assessment of child abuse or neglect should be shared on a 'need to know' basis in the interests of the child with the relevant statutory authorities.

No undertakings regarding secrecy can be given. Those working with a child and family should make this clear to all parties involved, although they can be assured that all information will be handled taking full account of legal requirements.

Ethical and statutory codes concerned with confidentiality and data protection provide general guidance. They are not intended to limit or prevent the exchange of information between professional staff with a responsibility for ensuring the protection and welfare of children. The provision of information to the statutory agencies for the protection of a child is not a breach of confidentiality or data protection.

It must be clearly understood that information gathered for one purpose must not be used for another without consulting the person who provided that information.

The issue of confidentiality should be part of the training necessary for staff who work in the area of child protection and welfare and the general training of staff in organisations that work with children. Each organisation should have a written policy in this regard.

Legal Protection

The Protections for Persons Reporting Child Abuse Act 1998 makes provision for the protection from civil liability of persons who have communicated child abuse 'reasonably and in good faith' to designated officers of the HSE or to any member of An Garda Síochána. This protection applies to organisations as well as to individuals. This means that even if a communicated suspicion of child abuse proves unfounded, a plaintiff who took an action would have to prove that the person who communicated the concern had not acted reasonably and in good faith in making the report.

A person who makes a report in good faith and in the child's best interests may also be protected under common law by the defence of qualified privilege.

Freedom of Information

Notwithstanding the requirement of all professionals involved in child protection and welfare cases to share relevant information, records are nevertheless confidential. They do not belong to individuals (except for independent practitioners) and are the property of the organisations that keep them. Under the Freedom of Information Acts 1997 and 2003, members of the public have a right of access to records concerning them held by any public body and a right to have official information about themselves amended where it is incorrect, incomplete or misleading. Members of the public also have a right to be given reasons for decisions made concerning themselves. Requests to see records are processed in the first instance through the public body that holds the records. In the event of refusal of access, the decision may be appealed and the ultimate arbiter is the Information

Commissioner. At present, these Acts apply to the HSE, but not to An Garda Síochána.

The Data Protection Acts 1988 and 2003 afford similar rights to individuals to access personal data held about them by any entity whether in the public or private sector. The right to access applies to records held by the HSE and An Garda Síochána. However, the right to access does not apply in a range of circumstances that may be relevant in a child welfare context. Equally, the right of access does not extend to any information that identifies a third party where that third party had an expectation of confidence. Accordingly, it would not be necessary to provide any information that would identify a person making a child welfare report in response to a request under the Data Protection Acts.

Those involved in childcare must remember, at all stages of their interactions with children in their care, that their own actions, or inactions, impact on a child's life, now and in the future. Bearing this in mind should encourage you to report any suspicions of abuse you may have.

Always remember that the children in your care depend on you and that when you chose your profession you undertook to follow the standards and ethics of that profession. This includes a duty to care; to support and protect the children in your charge and to put their interests and welfare above all other considerations.

CHAPTER 7

CHILDREN ACT 2001

Where the Child Care Act 1991 and the Children Act 2001 are referred to together they can be called the Child Care Acts 1991 and 2001.

The 2001 Act provides for additional procedures in relation to children, including:

- Regulation in relation to private foster care homes
- Inspections of private foster homes
- A system of diversion programmes, to be administered by An Garda Síochána, where a child between the age of criminal responsibility and eighteen accepts responsibility for a criminal wrongdoing and consents to the appointment of a juvenile liaison officer
- Issuing of formal and informal cautions to children
- Setting out the duties of An Garda Síochána in relation to underage children in custody
- The separation of children from adults while in custody
- Setting out the procedures and duties of the Children Court
- Use of parental supervision orders on parents where there is 'wilful failure of the child's parents to take care of or control the child'

- Use of day care orders, intensive care orders, detention centre and detention schools where appropriate.

Family Welfare Conferences

The Children Act 2001 allows for family conferences to facilitate the process of child protection. The Act sets out the procedures to be applied and allows that the following persons concerned with the child's welfare shall be entitled to attend:

(a)   the child in respect of whom the conference is being convened,

(b)   the parents or guardian of the child,

(c)   any guardian *ad litem* appointed for the child,

(d)   such other relative of the child as may be determined by the coordinator, after consultation with the child and the child's parents or guardian,

(e)   an officer or officers of the health board concerned,

(f)   any other person who, in the opinion of the coordinator, after consultation with the child and his or her parents or guardian, would make a positive contribution to the conference because of the person's knowledge of the child or the child's family or because of his or her particular expertise.

If, before or during a family welfare conference, the coordinator is of the opinion that the presence or continued presence of any person is not in the best interests of the conference or the child, the coordinator may exclude that person from participation or further participation in the conference.

Once again we see that the best interests of the child are to the forefront. Also, giving children the opportunity to be present, to have representation and to voice their opinions when things are being discussed about them is in line with Article 12 of the UN Convention on the Rights of the Child.

In defining the functions of a family welfare conference, the Act states that it will seek:

. . . to bring together the child in respect of whom the conference is being held, his or her parents or guardian, such other family members, relatives and other persons as appropriate and the facilitator with a view to—

(i)   establishing why the child became involved in the behaviour that gave rise to his or her admission to the Programme,

(ii)   discussing how the parents or guardian, family members, relatives or any other person could help to prevent the child from becoming involved in further such behaviour, and

(iii)   where appropriate, reviewing the child's behaviour since his or her admission to the Programme . . .

What is paramount in these situations is that the effort made by authorities gets the child into the best possible care situation in relation to that child's circumstances. The result of such conferences may be a special care order or a temporary or interim care order, which are allowed for in the Act.

Parental Supervision Orders

Under the 2001 Act, a parental supervision order may require the parents of the child to do any or all of the following:

(a)   to undergo treatment for alcohol or other substance abuse, where facilities for such treatment are reasonably available,

(b)   to participate in any course that is reasonably available for the improvement of parenting skills,

(c)   adequately and properly to control or supervise the child to the best of their ability, except where the terms of any community sanction imposed on the child make such control or supervision impracticable,

(d)   to comply with any other instructions of the court that would in its opinion assist in preventing the child from committing further offences.

A parental supervision order will be made for a period not exceeding six months. During that period the parents will be supported in their efforts to learn or correct things they may have been doing that may have resulted in the child's behaviour that was the reason for this process (always bearing in mind that the Constitution states that the child's place is in the family). The idea is that educating parents to provide a higher level of child supervision is probably fair in situations where those parents may have been neglected or abused themselves when they were children and may not actually have learnt what it is to be a good parent.

Supervision orders allow for some overview of the progress that is being made by all concerned and this support for the process of rehabilitation is very much in the child's best interests. It is clear to see that the essence of the Irish Constitution and the ideals set out in the UN Convention on the Rights of the Child have been taken seriously in these provisions.

CHAPTER 8

CHILD CARE (PRE-SCHOOL SERVICES) (NO. 2) REGULATIONS 2006

Some issues are dealt with by regulation rather than by the enactment of a law. Changes to a law must be passed by both Houses of the Oireachtas (the Dáil and the Seanad) and then signed and agreed to by the President, as outlined in the Constitution. This is often a lengthy process and open debate on small changes to operating conditions may result in further changes that restrict the potential effectiveness of the proposed amendment. The quicker way to change such detail is to put them in regulations, which are still binding but are more flexible in development and alteration.

The Child Care (Pre-School Services) (No. 2) Regulations 2006 provide for standards of service, upkeep and care for any setting defined as pre-school. The regulations define a pre-school child to be one under the age of six who is not in full-time education. Any person working with pre-school children must follow these regulations and they form part of the care contract for each child.

The contents of this book do not allow for a full analysis of every regulation contained in the Child

Care (Pre-School Services) (No. 2) Regulations 2006, however, all the regulations should be read properly in context to get a full understanding of the care and safety requirements that must be adhered to when running a childcare service. The regulations are there to protect children and to ensure the safety and welfare of each child. Inspections are carried out regularly to ensure that the required standards are maintained.

The remainder of this chapter focuses on some of the more significant details to be found in the regulations.

Carer/Child Ratios

The regulations changed the carer/child ratios that exist for different settings. The new ratios that came into effect are set out in the table opposite.

Additional changes have been made for childcare settings that have contracted to the ECCE scheme, but the ratios set out in the regulations are applicable in every other pre-school service.

This table does not reveal the full story in relation to the carer/child ratios as the regulations allow the Health Service Executive (HSE) to set a maximum number that can be cared for in a particular service – often this may happen because of space requirements.

Age Range	Carer/Child Ratio
Full or part-time day care service	
0 to 1 year	1:3
1 to 2 years	1:5
2 to 3 years	1:6
3 to 6 years	1:8
Sessional pre-school service	
0 to 1 year	1:3
1 to 2 years	1:5
2 to 6 years	1:10
Pre-school service in a drop-in centre or in a temporary drop-in centre*	
0 to 6 years full integration (spread)	1:4
Childminding service	
0 to 6 years	1:5 maximum, which would include own child, with conditions about the range of ages
Overnight pre-school service	
0 to 1 year	1:3
1 to 6 years	1:5

* Maximum group size is 24 and other detailed conditions apply.

Minimum Space Requirements

The regulations also specify a minimum space per child. The space requirements relate to clear floor space per child. Clear floor space means that area available for children's work, play and movement and does not include furniture that is surplus to the requirements of the child, or permanent fixtures. Places such as kitchens, toilets and sleeping or utility areas are not included in the space calculation in relation to a child.

Care of Children

The regulations set out specific requirements in relation to the care of children in pre-school facilities in order to protect the welfare of such children, including:

- A suitably equipped first-aid box for children must be kept on the premises
- Appropriate vetting of staff, students and volunteers who have access to children must be undertaken before they have access to a child in a pre-school service. In the case of a staff member this should refer to past employers; in relation to students and volunteers it should be by reference to reputable sources. Each case also includes Garda vetting
- No corporal punishment is allowed
- No disrespectful, degrading, exploitive, intimidating, emotionally or physically harmful or neglectful practices to be carried out in respect of any child

- Written policies and procedures must be in place in relation to challenging behaviour
- The HSE may set the maximum number of children that may be cared for in the space provided
- Proper insurance must be in place in each setting
- A register of children must be kept, recording the following details in respect of each child:
  - Name and date of birth
  - Date first attended the service
  - Date ceased to attend the service
  - Name and address and operation time telephone number of parent or guardian
  - Authorisation for collection
  - Details of illness, disability, allergy or special need
  - Name and telephone number of child's general practitioner
  - Record of immunisation
  - Written consent for appropriate medical treatment in emergencies
- Suitable heating, ventilation, light, sanitary accommodation, drainage, sewage disposal, waste disposal and storage must be provided in each pre-school facility
- Furniture must be adequate and work and play equipment must be of non-toxic materials, in a proper state of repair and in a clean and hygienic condition.

CHAPTER 9

MENTAL HEALTH ACT 2001

The Mental Health Act 2001 provides for the involuntary admission of patients suffering from mental disorders to approved centres of care. It also provides for review of such people and the establishment of a Mental Health Commission.

The Act defines a mental disorder as follows:

3. (1) In this Act 'mental disorder' means mental illness, severe dementia or significant intellectual disability where—

    (a) because of the illness, disability or dementia, there is a serious likelihood of the person concerned causing immediate and serious harm to himself or herself or to other persons, or

    (b) (i) because of the severity of the illness, disability or dementia, the judgment of the person concerned is so impaired that failure to admit the person to an approved centre would be likely to lead to a serious deterioration in his or her condition or would prevent the administration of appropriate treatment that could be given only by such admission, and

(ii) the reception, detention and treatment of the person concerned in an approved centre would be likely to benefit or alleviate the condition of that person to a material extent.

(2) In *subsection (1)*—

'mental illness' means a state of mind of a person which affects the person's thinking, perceiving, emotion or judgment and which seriously impairs the mental function of the person to the extent that he or she requires care or medical treatment in his or her own interest or in the interest of other persons;

'severe dementia' means a deterioration of the brain of a person which significantly impairs the intellectual function of the person thereby affecting thought, comprehension and memory and which includes severe psychiatric or behavioural symptoms such as physical aggression;

'significant intellectual disability' means a state of arrested or incomplete development of mind of a person which includes significant impairment of intelligence and social functioning and abnormally aggressive or seriously irresponsible conduct on the part of the person.

The Act goes further by saying in Section 4 that in the making of decisions under the Act for the care and treatment of a person (which might include admission to an approved centre) the best interests of the person shall be the principal consideration with due regard to the interests of other people who may be at risk of 'serious harm' if the decision is not made.

While it pre-dates the Disability Act 2005, which gives a more concise definition of disability, the Mental Health Act 2001 never envisaged that it would be used to detain people with intellectual disability which is not 'significant' as defined here. It is always important when reading any Act to check the definition section at the beginning of the Act to ascertain who it applies to and any technical definitions such as those above.

Involuntary Admission of Children

Section 23 of the Mental Health Act 2001 states that where the parents of a child, or indeed one of the parents or a person acting *in loco parentis,* wish to take a child who is a voluntary patient out of an approved centre and a registered medical prac-titioner, registered nurse on the centre's staff or a consultant psychiatrist is of the opinion that the child is suffering from a mental disorder as defined above, then the child may be kept and placed in the custody of the Health Service Executive (HSE).

It goes on to state that where this happens and the HSE wishes to detain the child under Section 25 of the Act (dealing with involuntary admission to approved centres) then the HSE must apply to the District Court for the area within three days of the child being taken into the HSE's care for such an involuntary detention order.

The granting in court of such an involuntary detention order under the Mental Health Act 2001 reflects the ideals of the UN Convention on the Rights of the Child, as under Section 25 of the Act the court requires specific details of the mental disorder claimed and, if satisfied that as the Act states:

(a)   the child is suffering from a mental disorder, and

(b)   the child requires treatment which he or she is unlikely to receive unless an order is made under this section,

then the HSE can apply to the District Court for an order of detention of the child in an approved centre and should only do so if a competent consultant psychiatrist (who is not a relation of the child) has examined the child and submitted a report. However, the Act also provides that if the parent(s) or somebody *in loco parentis* refuses to consent to the examination by the consultant psychiatrist or where no such person (parent or person acting *in loco parentis)* can be found then the HSE can apply without the prior examination of a consultant psychiatrist – the court can then direct that the examination takes place and that the report be brought to court within a specific period of time.

Where the court does receive this report within the time limit set, it will make an order for the child's detention for a period of not more than twenty-one days. Where such order has been made and the HSE wishes to extend it before it expires, the court may extend the period for three months and after that for a period not over six months, which may then be extended for further periods of six months if the court is satisfied that the child has been examined by a consultant psychiatrist who is not a relation of the child and that report is given to the court and the court after reading the report is satisfied the child is still suffering from a mental disorder.

Throughout this process, psycho-surgery and electro-convulsive therapy cannot be used on the child without the approval of the courts.

The Mental Health Act 2001 states that in all such proceedings Section 24 of the Child Care Act 1991 shall apply, which states that 'having regard to the rights and duties of parents, whether under the Constitution or otherwise', the court will:

a)   regard the welfare of the child as the first and paramount consideration, and

b)   in so far as is practicable, give due consideration, having regard to his age and understanding, to the wishes of the child.

This process is in line with the Convention on the Rights of the Child in that there is periodic review of the detention of the child and the best interests of the child will be taken into consideration.

There are two further issues in relation to children detained at approved centres under the Mental Health Act 2001:

Medicine

Medicine administered to a child in involuntary detention at an approved centre to relieve the mental disorder can only be given for a continuous period of three months unless the continuation of the medicine is either approved by the consultant psychiatrist responsible for the care of the child or approved (in a specific form determined by the Mental Health Commission) by another consultant psychiatrist after the matter has been referred to them by the consultant psychiatrist responsible for the care of the child. The procedure must be followed every three months so that authorisation and approval is obtained continuously.

Bodily Restraint and Seclusion

The Mental Health Commission makes rules regarding the use of mechanical means of restraint (such as seat belts) and seclusion of a patient. Such rules must be followed where it is deemed necessary 'for the purposes of treatment or to prevent the patient from injuring himself or herself or others'.

Throughout the Mental Health Act 2001, which was issued just after the Child Care Act 2001, the focus on the best interests of the child is evident and, while this is an emotive topic to deal with in relation to any child, the rules fulfil the ideals in the Convention on the Rights of the Child because of this principle and also because each detention is reviewed periodically, as is the administration of medicine.

CHAPTER 10

GUARDIANSHIP OF INFANTS ACT 1964

The Guardianship of Infants Act 1964, although pre-dating the Child Care Act 1991, affects some of the actions that can be taken in relation to children, particularly in relation to children who are born when their parents are not married. Indeed, the contents of the 1964 Act are sometimes unknown to the fathers of children until a problem arises.

One of the most important aspects of this Act is that it provides that the mother of a child born out of marriage is the automatic guardian of that child. The same automatic right does not apply to the father of such a child. Rather, the natural father must apply to the courts to be made a guardian of the child.

A father seeking to be made a guardian of his child must convince the court that he is prepared to protect the welfare of the child – this means the 'child's religious, moral, intellectual, physical and social welfare' (in other words, it is not just about making maintenance payments).

Where a guardian is appointed by will or deed (such as when the mother dies and appoints the natural father as guardian, also known as testamentary guardianship) and afterwards that person is deemed not to have the child's welfare as the first and paramount consideration then the courts can appoint a new guardian.

The Act allows the child to be consulted in relation to guardianship issues where appropriate.

Under the Act there is also a distinction between access and guardianship. A father can have access (the right to spend time with the child) and still not be the child's guardian. This could be relevant in legal issues that might arise in childcare.

A person working with children in any setting must understand that under the Guardianship of Infants Act 1964 a father may have lots of input into a child's care arrangements – such as seeing, delivering and collecting the child – but he may not be the child's guardian and cannot make decisions on the welfare of that child. It is important for legal reasons to know this distinction.

Some parents in modern relationships are not aware of this distinction and childcare workers should use diplomacy and tact when handling such cases.

If or when Article 42A of the Constitution is implemented there may be some changes to this situation. Article 42A refers to 'parents' and not 'guardians', and allows that parents may voluntarily elect to have their child adopted. Indeed if a parent fails to provide for a child for a period set out by law then the child can be adopted without the parent's consent – the Article does not state, in such cases, that the parent must also be the guardian. Additionally the child's opinion will be included in any consideration of such actions and their rights upheld.

CHAPTER 11

STATUS OF CHILDREN ACT 1987

The Status of Children Act 1987, which amended the Family Law (Maintenance of Spouses and Children) Act 1976, sought to define what exactly a family is in Irish legislation. Section 46 states:

(1) Where a woman gives birth to a child –

    (a) during a subsisting marriage to which she is a party, or

    (b) within the period of ten months after the termination, by death or otherwise, of a marriage to which she is a party,

then the husband of the marriage shall be presumed to be the father of the child unless the contrary is proved on the balance of probabilities.

In other words, in a married couple relationship it is usually presumed that the husband is the father of his wife's children unless otherwise proven.

(2) Notwithstanding *subsection (1)* of this section, where a married woman, being a woman who is living apart from her husband under –

(a)   a decree of divorce *a mensa et thoro*, or

(b)   a deed of separation,

gives birth to a child more than ten months after the decree was granted or the deed was executed as the case may be, then her husband shall be deemed not to be the father of the child unless the contrary is proved otherwise on the balance of probabilities.

In effect this means that where a couple separate by divorce or mutual separation, having been married, and a child is born *within* ten months of such separation or divorce then the ex-husband *is* presumed to be the father of the child unless otherwise proven.

(3)   Notwithstanding *subsection (1)* of this section, where –

(a)   the birth of a child is registered in a register maintained under the Births and Deaths Registration Acts, 1863 to 1987, and

(b)   the name of the person is entered as the father of the child on the register so maintained,

then the person whose name is entered shall be presumed to be the father of the child unless the contrary is proved on the balance of probabilities.

In other words, if the father is recorded as such on a legally correct register, then he is presumed to be the father unless otherwise proven.

Section 49 states:

(1)   In the case of a child whose parents were not married to each other at the date of his birth or at any time during the period of ten months before his birth, no person shall as father of the child be required to give information concerning the birth.

(2)   The registrar shall not enter in the register the name of a person as father of a child to whom subsection (1) of this section relates except –

(a)   at the joint request of the mother and the person acknowledging himself to be the father of the child, or

(b)   at the request of the mother on production of –

(i) a declaration in the prescribed form made by the mother stating that that person is the father of the child, and

(ii) a statutory declaration made by that person acknowledging himself to be the father of the child, or

(c)   at the request of that person on production of –

   (i) a declaration in the prescribed form by that person acknowledging himself to be the father of the child, and

   (ii) a statutory declaration made by the mother stating that that person is the father of the child,

or

(d)   at the request of the mother or that person, which shall in either case be made in writing , on production of a certified copy of any court order in respect of proceedings to which section 45 of the Status of Children Act 1987, relates, naming that person as the father of the child.

In essence, the father does not have to declare himself as the father if he does not want to and he cannot be forced to do so unless proper procedures are followed in law.

In relation to a child in a childcare setting, childcare workers should always ensure that they are informed about the policies and procedures of the setting in this regard.

CHAPTER 12

ADOPTION ACT 1988

The concept of the 'welfare of the child' is also a factor in the Adoption Act 1988, which provides that in exceptional cases where the parents for physical or moral reasons have failed in their duty to the child that child can be adopted by people who will take the place of those parents.

Section 3 of this Act states that the High Court can make an order for adoption of a child in extreme circumstances where it is satisfied

(I) that—

(A) for a continuous period of not less than 12 months immediately preceding the time of the making of the application, the parents of the child to whom the declaration under *section 2 (1)* relates, for physical or moral reasons, have failed in their duty towards the child,

(B) it is likely that such failure will continue without interruption until the child attains the age of 18 years,

(C) such failure constitutes an abandonment on the part of the parents of all parental rights, whether under the Constitution or otherwise, with respect to the child, and

(D)   by reason of such failure, the State, as guardian of the common good, should supply the place of the parents,

(II)   that the child—

(A)   at the time of the making of the application, is in the custody of and has a home with the applicants, and

(B)   for a continuous period of not less than 12 months immediately preceding that time, has been in the custody of and has had a home with the applicants,

and

(III)   that the adoption of the child by the applicants is an appropriate means by which to supply the place of the parents,

the Court may, if it so thinks fit and is satisfied, having had due regard for the rights, whether under the Constitution or otherwise, of the persons concerned (including the natural and imprescriptible rights of the child), that it would be in the best interests of the child to do so, make an order authorising the Board to make an adoption order in relation to the child in favour of the applicants.

(2) Before making an order under *subsection (1)*, the Court shall, in so far as is practicable, give due consideration, having regard to his age and understanding, to the wishes of the child concerned.

It needs to be emphasised that (until Article 42A of the Constitution is implemented) this applies in exceptional circumstances and that such actions are clearly based on the best interests of the child and comply with the constitutional rights of the child and indeed a parent's rights and duties to the child under the Constitution. It should not be assumed that the child is given away to strangers and there must already exist a situation where the child has been in the care of the adoptee parents for at least twelve months prior to such adoption. This can sometimes apply to the grandparents of the child in question, who may have taken over the care of the child due to their own child's inability or unwillingness to care for the moral welfare of the child.

If Article 42A comes into effect there will be a significant change in the application of the Adoption Act, and specifically the idea that Section 3 requires extreme circumstances to exist. There would no longer be the requirement that failure to provide for the child is expected to continue until the child reaches 18 years of age, as the Article allows for adoption after a period defined by law (which could change as the law is changed). The rights of the child to have their voice heard would still be included in any such move.

Additionally parents can opt for adoption voluntarily. This could considerably reduce the number of children in Ireland who live in foster homes because both parents have not agreed to adoption.

There are likely to be many changes to this Act if Article 42A becomes part of our Constitution, when the whole concept of adoption is likely to undergo a process of massive change.

CHAPTER 13

DOMESTIC VIOLENCE ACT 1996

Bearing in mind that a child witness of domestic violence will have suffered abuse by reason of the sight of the domestic violence, it is also necessary that childcare workers should have some grasp of the procedures in cases of domestic violence.

Under the Domestic Violence Act 1996 there are a number of orders that can be obtained in cases of domestic violence.

Safety Orders

A safety order stops the person carrying on the violent act from doing more or threatening violence against the person being abused. Provided there are reasonable grounds for thinking the person's safety or welfare is at risk, safety orders are available to the following:

- A husband or wife who is being subjected to violence – remember it is both men and women – can apply on their own behalf or on behalf of a child
- If a couple are not married and have lived together for six months of the last twelve months, then the abused partner can apply
- A parent can get one against an adult child

- A person who has a non-contractual relationship and lives with the other person – not a lodger or tenant
- Relatives who live together can get an order against each other if necessary
- The Health Service Executive (HSE) can apply on somebody's behalf.

Barring Orders

A barring order requires the violent person to leave and not re-enter the family home, not use threatening behaviour, not molest and not be in the area where the person lives for the duration of the barring order or up to three years unless it has been extended beyond that by the Circuit Court. Barring orders are available to the following:

- A husband or wife who is being subjected to violence can apply on their own behalf or on behalf of a child
- A couple who are not married, own part of the house in question and have lived together for six of the previous nine months, then the abused partner can apply
- A parent of a grown child unless the child owns or has greatest ownership of the house
- The Health Service Executive (HSE).

Protection Orders

A protection order is made until the outcome of a safety order or barring order procedure is known and is only of temporary duration. It may be given in cases where there is a belief that the person is in immediate danger. It can be made without the knowledge of the person committing the violence (*ex parte*) but in such cases the person must be notified immediately and a court hearing should take place involving the excluded person within eight working days of the order being granted.

While these procedures may mean the child is effectively deprived of one parent or significant adult, it is because it is in the child's best interests to remove the perpetrator.

CHAPTER 14

DATA PROTECTION ACTS 1988 AND 2003

Where information is held about a family or child in a childcare setting it is subject to the Data Protection Acts of 1988 and 2003.

The Data Protection Act 1988 restricts the use of 'personal data', which means 'data relating to a living individual who can be identified either from the data or from the data in conjunction with other information in the possession of the data collector'.

The Act states that data collected on a person:

- Should be fairly gained
- Should be accurate and up to date
- Should be kept for only one or more specified lawful purposes
- Shall not be disclosed in other circumstances
- Shall be adequate, relevant and not excessive
- Shall not be kept longer than necessary to fulfil its purposes.

The Act also specifies that the person holding the data must have adequate security in place to protect the data and there should be no unauthorised access to the data, which cannot be altered, destroyed or disclosed without the person's permission.

A person is entitled under the Act to request to know if such data exists about them and, on the payment of a nominal fee, to be given a copy of such data within forty days. Where the information is found to be false or mistaken, the person is entitled to have such errors or mistakes rectified.

A person working with children should always be aware that such a request can be made on behalf of a child in their care and should ensure that information kept is adequate and not excessive for the protection of the best interests of the child.

More importantly, childcare workers should respect the privacy and confidentiality of any information given to them in relation to any child in the childcare setting and also be aware that there are fines for breaches of the Data Protection Acts.

Children First: National Guidance for the Protection and Welfare of Children (2011) explains that there is no requirement to disclose the identity of a person who has made a child protection report unless that person was aware that this might happen. It effectively considers an exception to the Data Protection Acts, and when the guidance is given a legislative footing, as is expected, this is likely to be included in any legislation.

CHAPTER 15

OMBUDSMAN FOR CHILDREN ACT 2002

The Ombudsman for Children Act 2002 established the post of Ombudsman for Children and provided that such office should be independent. Furthermore, the Ombudsman is charged with performing his or her duty having regard to 'the best interests of the child' concerned and in so far as practicable should give due consideration, having regard to the age and understanding of the child, to his or her wishes. A child under the Act is somebody under eighteen years of age, except where the person is enlisted with the Defence Forces.

As this book illustrates, the best interests of the child are central to the protection of children's rights under the Constitution, although these rights are not actually specified. This Act also employs the familiar expression 'in so far as is practicable', which basically means that other factors may militate against the application of these ideals.

The Act charges the Ombudsman for Children with the promotion of the rights and welfare of children, which includes:

- Advising government ministers on the development and co-ordination of policy relating to children

- Encouraging public bodies, schools and voluntary hospitals to develop policies, practices and procedures designed to promote the rights and welfare of children
- Collecting and disseminating information on matters relating to the rights and welfare of children
- Promoting awareness among members of the public (including children of appropriate age) on matters relating to the rights and welfare of the child, including the UN Convention on the Rights of the Child
- Highlighting issues of concern to children in relation to their rights and welfare
- Co-operating and exchanging information with the Ombudsman for Children (or equivalent post) in other states
- Monitoring and reviewing generally the operation of legislation concerning matters that relate to the rights and welfare of children
- Monitoring and reviewing the operation of the Ombudsman for Children Act 2002.

The ideals of the Convention on the Rights of the Child are very much the starting point of this piece of legislation and the Act further charges the Ombudsman with setting up structures to consult regularly with groups of children considered by the Ombudsman to be representative of children. In such consultations the views of the child are to be given due weight in accordance with the age and understanding of the child.

The Ombudsman for Children is appointed by the President after the resolution (agreement) of the Dáil and the Seanad and holds office for a period of six years, which can be renewed once only (i.e. the maximum period that can be served is twelve years). The Ombudsman may be removed from office (at his or her request or for reasons stated in the Act) by the President, again on the resolution of both Houses of the Oireachtas.

CHAPTER 16

EDUCATION (WELFARE) ACT 2000

The Education (Welfare) Act 2000 provides for the entitlement of every child in the state to a certain minimum education, whether that is in a recognised school or otherwise provided (such as home schooling). A minimum standard of education was also set as an ideal in the Constitution under Article 42.2 and in the UN Convention on the Rights of the Child under Articles 28 and 29.

For the purposes of this Act a child refers to 'a person resident in the State who has reached the age of 6 years and who (*a*) has not reached the age of 16 years, or (*b*) has not completed 3 years of post-primary education, whichever occurs later, but shall not include a person who has reached the age of 18 years'.

The Act established the National Educational Welfare Board, which is charged with the implementation of the detail of the Act, including:

(a) to promote and foster in society, and in particular in families, an appreciation of the benefits to be derived from education, in particular as respects the physical, intellectual, emotional, social, cultural and moral development of children, and of the social and economic advantages that flow therefrom,

(b)   to promote and foster, in recognised schools, an environment that encourages children to attend school and participate fully in the life of the school,

(c)   to conduct and commission research into the reasons for non-attendance on the part of students and into strategies and programmes designed to prevent it,

(d)   to disseminate to recognised schools the findings of research conducted or commissioned pursuant to paragraph (c), and to advise such schools on matters relating to the prevention of non-attendance, and the good conduct of students generally,

(e)   to assist recognised schools in so far as is practicable to meet their obligations under this Act,

(f)   to advise and assist children and the parents of children who exhibit problems relating to attendance at, and behaviour in, school,

(g)   to support, monitor, and assess the effectiveness of, strategies and programmes aimed at preventing non-attendance in recognised schools,

(h)   to cooperate with such persons as the Board considers appropriate, and to coordinate the activities of the Board with the activities of those persons in so far as they relate to preventing non-attendance in recognised schools,

(i)   to carry out reviews of training and guidance given to teachers relating to matters of school attendance and the conduct of students, and to advise the Minister in relation thereto,

(j)   to advise the National Council for Curriculum and Assessment as respects those aspects of the school curriculum that, in the opinion of the Board, are likely to have an effect on attendance levels at, or the extent of student participation in, school, and

(k)   to advise the Minister on any matter to which this Act relates.

Interestingly, the Act requires the National Educational Welfare Board to have due regard to the cost of the measures it proposes, which could be interpreted as putting a financial limit on the best interests of the child.

Behavioural aspects in school form a part of the Act's provisions and in situations where behaviour may indicate other underlying problems the Act allows for investigations to take place in relation to that behaviour. The National Educational Welfare Board can, with the agreement of parents, arrange for a child to be assessed. Where such consent is not given by the parents, the board can apply to the Circuit Court for an order that the assessment takes place when the Circuit Court agrees that it appears necessary for such assessment to take place.

The Act allows for the appointment of educational welfare officers, who are appointed by warrant which can be produced when exercising their functions (again in keeping with the ideals expressed in both the Irish Constitution and the UN Convention on the Rights of the Child). The board can assign additional functions to such officers outside of those specified in the Act.

The Act requires a register to be kept of every child who is receiving education other than in a recognised establishment and to have that standard ascertained to ensure that the child in question is receiving a minimum standard of education. Where this is not the case, the standard must be increased.

It does not state that this requirement is in the child's best interests and indeed the child may by definition require much more than the minimum (particularly if the child is gifted or talented) but this is not dealt with in the Act even though it could affect the child's performance, attendance and behaviour.

The Act provides that parents or guardians must ensure that where children do attend recognised schools they must attend regularly and that in the case of unwarranted absences parents can be held liable for non-attendance, which can mean a fine and/or imprisonment.

CHAPTER 17

EDUCATION FOR PERSONS WITH SPECIAL EDUCATIONAL NEEDS ACT 2004

The Education for Persons with Special Educational Needs Act 2004 (also known as the EPSEN Act) is a very important step in realising the goal of equality in relation to education for people with special needs. The Act also provides for the setting up of the National Council for Special Education and sets out how decisions may be appealed. The Act had not been fully implemented when it was effectively suspended by the 2008 Budget – the aim was to bring the Act into operation over ten years but this, while not negated, has been frustrated or delayed.

The Act states that 'special educational needs' refers to 'a restriction in the capacity of the person to participate in and benefit from education on account of an enduring physical, sensory, mental health or learning disability, or any other condition which results in a person learning differently from a person without that condition'. The Act provides that:

> A child with special educational needs shall be educated in an inclusive environment with children who do not have such needs unless the

nature or degree of those needs of the child is such that to do so would be inconsistent with—

(a) the best interests of the child as determined in accordance with any assessment carried out under this Act, or

(b) the effective provision of education for children with whom the child is to be educated.

It should be noted that this is a provision with a tail – in other words, exceptions can be made to inclusive education, specifically where it might interfere with a child's ability to participate where that child has no special need.

The Act puts responsibility on a school principal where the parents inform the principal that they are of the opinion that the child is not benefiting as much as would be expected from what is being offered in the school or where the principal forms this view and may believe that this is because the child may have special needs. In such cases the principal must arrange to have the student assessed within a month of forming that view. The assessment must be completed within three months of the formation of the view (i.e. within two months of the start of the assessment). Guidelines for such assessment will be provided by the National Council for Special Education.

If the child is assessed (the Act specifies who would be suitably qualified to carry out such an assessment) as having special needs, the principal must have a plan prepared for the appropriate education of that child within one month of receiving this confirmation. This plan is called an IEP or Individual Educational Plan for the child. It must be drawn up in consultation with the parents and teachers if appropriate. The principal must give written notice of such a plan to the parents and give them a copy of the plan.

In the case of a child whose special needs are such that an IEP prepared by the school would not meet the needs of the child or where an IEP already prepared is not meeting the needs of the child, the principal must request the National Council for Special Education to prepare an education plan.

The Health Service Executive (HSE) may also arrange an assessment of a child where it forms the view that the child may have special needs whether a student or not.

Parents are required to be consulted throughout this process but where parents refuse to agree to an assessment the Circuit Court may do so in the best interests of the child.

The plan should include:

- The type and extent of the child's abilities, skills and talents
- The type and extent of the child's special educational needs and how they affect the child's educational development

- The level of the child's current educational performance
- The child's special educational needs (i.e. what can be offered in such cases)
- The supports needed to ensure that the child benefits from education
- Where necessary, the supports the child needs to make the change from pre-school to primary school
- Similarly, the supports the child needs to make the move from primary to secondary school
- The goals the child should achieve over a period of not more than one year.

The principal is responsible for putting the prepared plan into action. The principal must review the plan at least once a year to ensure that the services specified in the plan were received and the goals of the plan were met. If the parents feel that a review is necessary and one has not taken place in the previous six months they may make a request for a review to be done and the principal must inform the parents if one is not done. The Act also specifies that if the child moves school, then the principal must let the principal of the new school know that a plan exists before a transfer takes place.

Childcare workers should be aware that a child may have an IEP in place and activities undertaken in relation to that child should follow the procedures, methods and goals of the plan. Such children have a right to expect that all people working with them are aware of and follow their IEP.

Once again the value of observation is important in this regard as not everybody will inform you about the fact that a child may have a 'special need' and you may indeed be the first to observe the need for a possible assessment of such special need.

CHAPTER 18

DISABILITY ACT 2005

The Disability Act 2005 defines a disability in relation to a person as meaning:

> . . . a substantial restriction in the capacity of the person, which is permanent or likely to be permanent, to carry on a profession, business or occupation in the State or to participate in social or cultural life in the State by reason of an enduring physical, sensory, mental health or intellectual impairment.

The Act provides similar provisions to those that apply in the Education for Persons with Special Educational Needs Act 2004 but there is an Assessment of Need Report rather than an IEP.

The Assessment of Need Report will include:

- Whether a person has a disability
- The nature and extent of the disability
- The health and education needs arising from the disability
- The services considered appropriate to meet those needs and the timescale ideally required for their delivery
- When a review of assessment should take place.

The person with the disability will be involved with the process and in some cases the Health Service Executive (HSE) can initiate the assessment on behalf of a person.

Children with a disability can be assessed under the Disability Act 2005 or under the Education for Persons with Special Educational Needs Act 2004 as there may be special needs as a result of the disability. Where this happens, then that aspect of the assessment is notified to the National Council for Special Education or to the principal of the school the child attends.

The Disability Act 2005 also stipulates appeal procedures where a person is not satisfied with the procedure, and these are heard by a complaints officer.

The Act also:

- Provides that people with disabilities should have access to public buildings, services and information
- Establishes sectoral plans for six government departments to ensure that services for people with disabilities are integrated into planning and provision
- Establishes a duty on public bodies to be proactive in employing people with disabilities
- Prohibits the use of genetic testing for employment, mortgage or insurance purposes
- Establishes a Centre for Excellence in Universal Design.

One possible flaw with the Act is that while it says equality of access should be available for persons with disability, it excludes some places where it is considered not to be practicable or justifiable on cost grounds or where there would be unreasonable delay in doing so – this may leave some doors still closed to people on the basis of cost or delay and it does not say who would judge whether such an exception would be reasonable.

CHAPTER 19

CRIMINAL JUSTICE ACT 2006

As can be expected in any society, there are occasions when children in Ireland find themselves on the wrong side of the law. The Criminal Justice Act 2006 has made significant changes to the way such instances are dealt with.

The Act changed the age of criminal responsibility in relation to a child to twelve (except in the case of murder, manslaughter, rape or aggravated assault when a child is aged ten or eleven). It directs that in its dealings 'with a child charged with an offence, a court shall have due regard to the child's best interests, the interests of the victim of the offence and the protection of society'. Here we see that a triangulated view of the best interests of the child is taken and indeed throughout the Act the use of the phrase 'best interests of the child' is sparse to say the least.

Many of the measures included in the Act are new to the Irish situation, for example behaviour orders, and the wording in these sections is based on a belief that children must accept responsibility for their actions and agree to change the behaviour that caused the problem.

The Act provides for assistance to be given to children in relation to legal proceedings against them, and states that where they are detained they should be detained separately from adults (as would be the case in St Patrick's Institution for instance) except where it would not be in the child's best interests to do so.

While the wording of the Act may be terse, as one might expect in relation to criminal matters, the concepts outlined in the UN Convention on the Rights of the Child are present such as children's rights to representation, to timely administration of justice, to challenge their detention and to have matters they raise dealt with by an impartial authority.

The notion of 'evolving capacities' is also incorporated into the Act in Section 124, which provides:

> Where a child under 14 years of age is charged with an offence, the Court may, of its own motion or the application of any person, dismiss the case on its merits if, having had due regard to the child's age and level of maturity, it determines that the child did not have a full understanding of what was involved in the commission of the offence.

Another important aspect of the Criminal Justice Act 2006 is the introduction in Section 176 of the criminal charge of reckless endangerment of children, where it states:

> A person, having authority or control over a child or abuser, who intentionally or recklessly endangers a child by –

(a)   causing or permitting any child to be placed or left in a situation which creates a substantial risk to the child of being a victim of serious harm or sexual abuse, or

(b)   failing to take reasonable steps to protect a child from such a risk while knowing that the child is in such a situation, is guilty of an offence.

This has major implications in ensuring that people take what they do in relation to children very seriously. This criminal charge is the very basis on which a decision to report child protection concerns should be made, as not to report your concern could mean that you have recklessly endangered the child under this Act.

The penalty for a person found guilty of this offence is a fine (with no upper limit) and/or imprisonment for a term not exceeding ten years. Even if there were no conviction an allegation under this Act could lead to 'soft' information about you being exchanged with the National Vetting Bureau. It is therefore imperative to ensure that you do the right thing when working with children and put yourself and your professionalism beyond reproach.

CHAPTER 20

CHILD CARE (AMENDMENT) ACT 2007

The Child Care (Amendment) Act 2007 relates to children who have been in the care of the same foster or relative family for five years or more. It might appear on first reading that this is similar to the Adoption Act 1988, however, it differs significantly in that it does not relate to adoption by the people who have been looking after the child but merely puts them in a place as if they were the parents where that is in the child's best interests.

The courts can make an order to allow the qualifying relative or foster parent:

(a)   to have, on behalf of the Health Service Executive, the like control over the child as if the foster parent or relative were the child's parent, and

(b)   to do, on behalf of the Health Service Executive, what is reasonable (subject to the provisions of this Act and of the regulations for the time being in force under this Act) in all the circumstances of the case for the purpose of safeguarding and promoting the child's health, development or welfare and, in particular, give consent to—

(i) any necessary medical or psychiatric examination, treatment or assessment with respect to the child, and

(ii) the issue of a passport to, or the provision of passport facilities for, the child to enable the child to travel abroad for a limited period.

Under the Act the courts must be satisfied that:

(a) the foster parent or relative has been taking care of the child for a period of not less than five years beginning on the date of placement in accordance with this Act and ending on the date of application,

(b) the granting of the order is in the child's best interests,

(c) the Health Service Executive has consented in advance to the granting of the order,

(d) the Health Service Executive has, on behalf of the foster parent or relative—

(i) if the child is in its care under section 4, obtained the consent to the granting of the order of a parent having custody of the child at the relevant time or of a person (other than the foster parent or relative) acting *in loco parentis* to the child, or

(ii) if the child is in its care under section 18, given notice of the application to a parent having custody of the child at the relevant time or of a person (other than the foster parent or relative) acting *in loco parentis* to the child, and

(e)   the child's wishes have, in so far as is practicable, been given due consideration having regard to the age and understanding of the child.

The Act provides that the consent of the parent included above does not apply if:

(a)   the court is satisfied that he or she is missing and cannot be found by the Health Service Executive, or

(b)   the court, having regard to the child's welfare, so directs.

An order under the Act can be conditional and can be reversed (as outlined in the Act), which is where the central difference between this Act and the Adoption Act 1988 lies. The purpose of placing the temporary carer in the position of the parent in the Child Care (Amendment) Act 2007 is to allow permission to be given for medical treatment, including but not just restricted to psychiatric treatment. Similarly, it would never be in the child's best interests to be the only child in a whole school not to go on a foreign trip, for instance, just because the foster parents or foster relatives could not provide the necessary permissions needed to get a passport to travel out of the country.

Should Article 42A be incorporated into our Constitution, changes to this Act are likely to be effected. Article 42A may well allow children to be adopted in circumstances where this Act would otherwise apply. This might arise in cases where a parent cannot be found to give consent. In such circumstances it is likely that the provisions of Article 42A, if incorporated into law, would allow for a different outcome for the child in question.

CHAPTER 21

PASSPORTS ACT 2008

The Passports Act 2008 allows the Minister for Foreign Affairs to authorise the issuing of a passport to a child where the minister is 'satisfied on reasonable grounds that each person who is a guardian of the child consents to the issue of a passport to the child'.

We saw that one factor that was relevant in the Child Care (Amendment) Act 2007, was the requirement that the child in question had been in the care of the foster or relative carer family for a period of five years. However, there are often situations where the issuing of a passport for a child can also prove problematic and the Passports Act tries to include those situations.

Section 14 of the Act allows the Minister for Foreign Affairs, on the application of only one guardian, to issue a passport for a child where perhaps one parent lives abroad with the child:

(a)   having regard to all the circumstances of the case, including whether or not that other guardian of the child has notified the Minister in writing that he or she objects to the issue of a passport to the child, and

(b)   for the purpose of securing the welfare of the child

This provision might be used to facilitate the return of the child or assist in proceedings to have the child repatriated in some situations.

The minister can also issue a passport with the consent of one guardian, or indeed no guardian, where the application is made by somebody who has an interest in the welfare of the child and the minister is satisfied:

(a) there exist in relation to the child exceptional circumstances involving an immediate and serious risk of harm to his or her life, health or safety requiring him or her to undertake travel for which a passport is required, and

(b) for the purpose of securing the welfare of the child.

All these conditions could be seen as facilitating children to have access to their family and indeed to their nationality and identity as required under the UN Convention on the Rights of the Child. The ability of the minister to put the child's welfare above the guardian's permission may be essential in some situations where families are scattered throughout the world but such situations would be dealt with on an individual case basis.

The Act states that guardians who give their permission will be taken to have agreed indefinitely unless they communicate their change of mind to the minister in writing (this might stop a vexatious situation where separation might have taken place after the permission was originally given, as has happened).

The Passports Act 2008 is another Act which could be affected, if not directly by Article 42A, then possibly by its implications in practice. The idea that children should have better outcomes and that their best interests would be taken into account is likely to ensure that unreasonableness in giving permission for a passport would not necessarily prove as big a stumbling block as it has to date.

CHAPTER 22

CRIMINAL JUSTICE (WITHHOLDING OF INFORMATION ON OFFENCES AGAINST CHILDREN AND VULNERABLE PERSONS) ACT 2012

This Act was passed to ensure that persons who were in receipt of information relating to the commission of certain offences, including sexual offences, against children and vulnerable persons would report such information. It provides that a person will be guilty of an offence if

(a)   he or she knows or believes that an offence, that is a Schedule 1 offence, has been committed by another person against a child, and

(b)   he or she has information which he or she knows or believes might be of material assistance in securing the apprehension, prosecution or conviction of that other person for that offence, and fails without reasonable excuse to disclose that information as soon as it is practicable to do so to a member of the Garda Síochána.

The penalty for not disclosing material information is set out at section 7 and includes

(a)   on summary conviction, to a class A fine or imprisonment for a term not exceeding 12 months or both, or

(b)   on conviction on indictment, to a fine or imprisonment or both according to the gravity of the Schedule 1 offence or Schedule 2 offence, as the case may be, concerned in respect of which the person failed to disclose information that he or she had as soon as it was practicable to do so to a member of the Garda Síochána, in the following manner:

(i)   if the Schedule 1 offence or Schedule 2 offence, as the case may be, concerned is one for which the maximum sentence is imprisonment for life, he or she shall be liable to imprisonment for a term not exceeding 10 years;

(ii)   if it is one for which a person of full capacity and not previously convicted may be sentenced to imprisonment for a term of 14 years, he or she shall be liable to imprisonment for a term not exceeding 7 years;

(iii)   if it is not one included in subparagraph (i) or (ii) but is one for which a person of full capacity and not previously convicted may be sentenced to imprisonment for a term of 10 years, he or she shall be liable to imprisonment for a term not exceeding 5 years;

(iv)   in any other case, he or she shall be liable to imprisonment for a term not exceeding 3 years.

If nothing else these penalties should instil in everybody working with children and vulnerable persons that they should take very seriously their responsibilities in relation to their protection. The Children First Bill 2012, which has been put on hold until a decision on Article 42A is made, proposed in its first draft that the designated reporting person in every organisation should be make criminally liable for non-disclosure of information in relation to a child protection issue in their setting. This might well have been a reflection of the penalties of this Act, and if that were so, then the implications of getting it wrong or doing nothing would be enormous.

CHAPTER 23

THE BEST INTERESTS OF THE CHILD

As this book has illustrated, the expression 'the best interests of the child' is widely used and is a fundamental concept in the treatment of children in the Irish legal system, and indeed under the UN Convention on the Rights of the Child. The best interests of the child is an outcome which the Thirty-First Amendment of the Constitution (Children) Bill 2012 was intended to enshrine in our Constitution, but it has unfortunately been put on hold in relation to its implementation in the Constitution. While we are led to believe that it is some part of giving children equal rights under our Constitution, it is unfortunate that in so doing we did not have regard to the idea that such a right should be inalienable and therefore incapable of being removed, transferred or altered.

In defining what exactly the best interests of the child are, it is useful to note that the word 'interests' is plural but the word 'child' is singular. It reminds us to relate to the child as an individual and not as part of a group setting. Each situation must be dealt with individually and the solutions found should take account of each individual child.

The child must be put at the centre of decisions

made concerning that particular child to achieve the best possible outcome in relation to that child. In so far as it is possible the child must be allowed to express his or her opinion in relation to such deliberations according to his or her 'evolving capacities' as stated in the Convention on the Rights of the Child. This probably also means that the solution should be reviewed as the child evolves – an interesting concept not yet addressed in the Irish system (with the possible exception of the Mental Health Act 2001).

The concept of the best decision in relation to the individual child was investigated by a South African Constitutional Court Judge, Albie Sachs, in the case of *M v. The State* (Case CCT 53/06 [2007] ZACC18). Judge Sachs had to decide on an option of the courts in South Africa to jail a mother over repeated fraud offences despite leniency of sentencing in previous cases. The judge held that in the circumstances of the mother's children and their best interests it was not appropriate to activate a jail sentence for the woman as her children might be put at risk and that a more appropriate punishment would be community service where she could still look after her children and thus protect their interests.

This topic was also examined in a report by Scotland's Commissioner for Children and Young People, Kathleen Marshall, published in February 2008, called *Not Seen. Not Heard. Not Guilty. The Rights and Status of the Children of Prisoners in*

Scotland. The report considered the effect on children when a parent is imprisoned and pointed out that it did not always have a negative impact as in some cases the child could be very relieved that the parent has been imprisoned and may feel safer as a result. It is clear that there is no one-fits-all solution, rather a consideration of all elements of the individual child's life should be taken into account when decisions are made. Indeed Marshall pointed out that this is not always easy either, as when some children feel very vulnerable it can be hard to find out their views and 'children will often tell ChildLine things they would not tell anyone else'.

To secure the best interests of the child we must take a child-centred approach to all dealings with children. In the words of Judge Sachs:

> ... every child has his or her own dignity. If a child is to be constitutionally imagined as an individual with a distinctive personality, and not merely as a miniature adult waiting to reach full size, he or she cannot be treated as a mere extension of his or her parents, umbilically destined to sink or swim with them.

A child-centred focus allows the child to grow into the best possible adult he or she is capable of being and this requires some assistance along the way from the people who come into contact with that child in whatever capacity.

As a person working with children you must be aware of the effect of every aspect of your behaviour on the children in your care. You must listen to the opinions of the children in your care and give due consideration to those opinions, bearing in mind the child's evolving capacities, and you must provide a voice for children who cannot articulate for themselves. In every aspect of your work you are charged with the protection of the children in your care from abuse, neglect and exploitation. You are also responsible for ensuring that each child in your care develops to his or her best potential in a safe and nurturing environment, bearing in mind the words of Judge Sachs:

> Individually and collectively all children have the right to express themselves as independent social beings, to have their own laughter as well as sorrow, to play, to imagine and explore in their own way, to themselves get to understand their bodies, minds and emotions, and above all to learn as they grow how they should conduct themselves and make choices in the wide social and moral world of adulthood. And foundational to the enjoyment of the right to childhood is the promotion of the right as far as possible to live in a secure and nurturing environment free from violence, fear, want and avoidable trauma.

SIGNS AND SYMPTOMS OF CHILD ABUSE

From *Children First: National Guidance for the Protection and Welfare of Children* (2011)

1. Signs and symptoms of neglect

Child neglect is the most common category of abuse. A distinction can be made between 'wilful' neglect and 'circumstantial' neglect. 'Wilful' neglect would generally incorporate a direct and deliberate deprivation by a parent/carer of a child's most basic needs, e.g. withdrawal of food, shelter, warmth, clothing, contact with others. 'Circumstantial' neglect more often may be due to stress/inability to cope by parents or carers.

Neglect is closely correlated with low socio-economic factors and corresponding physical deprivations. It is also related to parental incapacity due to learning disability, addictions or psychological disturbance.

The neglect of children is 'usually a passive form of abuse involving omission rather than acts of commission' (Skuse and Bentovim, 1994). It comprises 'both a lack of physical caretaking and supervision and a failure to fulfil the developmental needs of the child in terms of cognitive stimulation'.

Child neglect should be suspected in cases of:

- abandonment or desertion;
- children persistently being left alone without adequate care and supervision;
- malnourishment, lacking food, inappropriate food or erratic feeding;
- lack of warmth;
- lack of adequate clothing;
- inattention to basic hygiene;
- lack of protection and exposure to danger, including moral danger or lack of supervision appropriate to the child's age;
- persistent failure to attend school;
- non-organic failure to thrive, i.e. child not gaining weight due not only to malnutrition but also to emotional deprivation;
- failure to provide adequate care for the child's medical and developmental problems;
- exploited, overworked.

2. Characteristics of neglect

Child neglect is the most frequent category of abuse, both in Ireland and internationally. In addition to being the most frequently reported type of abuse; neglect is also recognised as being the most harmful. Not only does neglect generally last throughout a childhood, it also has long-term consequences into adult life. Children are more likely to die from chronic neglect than from one instance of physical abuse. It is well established that severe neglect in infancy has a serious negative impact on brain development.

Neglect is associated with, but not necessarily caused by, poverty. It is strongly correlated with parental substance misuse, domestic violence and parental mental illness and disability.

Neglect may be categorised into different types (adapted from Dubowitz, 1999):

- Disorganised/chaotic neglect: This is typically where parenting is inconsistent and is often found in disorganised and crisis-prone families. The quality of parenting is inconsistent, with a lack of certainty and routine, often resulting in emergencies regarding accommodation, finances and food. This type of neglect results in attachment disorders, promotes anxiety in children and leads to disruptive and attention-seeking behaviour, with older children proving more difficult to control and discipline. The home may be unsafe from accidental harm, with a high incident of accidents occurring.

- Depressed or passive neglect: This type of neglect fits the common stereotype and is often characterised by bleak and bare accommodation, without material comfort, and with poor hygiene and little if any social and psychological stimulation. The household will have few toys and those that are there may be broken, dirty or inappropriate for age. Young children will spend long periods in cots, playpens or pushchairs. There is often a lack of food, inadequate bedding and no clean clothes. There can be a sense of hopelessness, coupled with ambivalence about improving the household situation. In such environments, children frequently are absent from school and have poor homework routines. Children subject to these circumstances are at risk of major developmental delay.

- Chronic deprivation: This is most likely to occur where there is the absence of a key attachment figure. It is most often found in large institutions where infants and children may be physically well cared for, but where there is no opportunity to form an attachment with an individual carer. In these situations, children are dealt with by a range of adults and their needs are seen as part of the demands of a group of children. This form of deprivation will also be associated with poor stimulation and can result in serious developmental delays.

The following points illustrate the consequences of different types of neglect for children:

- inadequate food – failure to develop;
- household hazards – accidents;
- lack of hygiene – health and social problems;
- lack of attention to health – disease;
- inadequate mental health care – suicide or delinquency;
- inadequate emotional care – behaviour and educational;
- inadequate supervision – risk-taking behaviour;
- unstable relationship – attachment problems;
- unstable living conditions – behaviour and anxiety, risk of accidents;
- exposure to domestic violence – behaviour, physical and mental health;
- community violence – anti-social behaviour.

3. Signs and symptoms of emotional neglect and abuse

Emotional neglect and abuse is found typically in a home lacking in emotional warmth. It is not necessarily associated with physical deprivation. The emotional needs of the children are not met; the parent's relationship to the child may be without empathy and devoid of emotional responsiveness.

Emotional neglect and abuse occurs when adults responsible for taking care of children are unaware of and unable (for a range of reasons) to meet their children's emotional and developmental needs. Emotional neglect and abuse is not easy to recognise because the effects are not easily observable. Skuse (1989) states that 'emotional abuse refers to the habitual verbal harassment of a child by disparagement, criticism, threat and ridicule, and the inversion of love, whereby verbal and non-verbal means of rejection and withdrawal are substituted'.

Emotional neglect and abuse can be identified with reference to the indices listed below. However, it should be noted that no one indicator is conclusive of emotional abuse. In the case of emotional abuse and neglect, it is more likely to impact negatively on a child where there is a cluster of indices, where these are persistent over time and where there is a lack of other protective factors:

- rejection;
- lack of comfort and love;
- lack of attachment;
- lack of proper stimulation (e.g. fun and play);

- lack of continuity of care (e.g. frequent moves, particularly unplanned);
- continuous lack of praise and encouragement;
- serious over-protectiveness;
- inappropriate non-physical punishment (e.g. locking in bedrooms);
- family conflicts and/or violence;
- every child who is abused sexually, physically or neglected is also emotionally abused;
- inappropriate expectations of a child relative to his/her age and stage of development.

Children who are physically and sexually abused and neglected also suffer from emotional abuse.

4. Signs and symptoms of physical abuse

Unsatisfactory explanations, varying explanations, frequency and clustering for the following events are high indices for concern regarding physical abuse:

- bruises (see below for more detail);
- fractures;
- swollen joints;
- burns/scalds (see below for more detail);
- abrasions/lacerations;
- haemorrhages (retinal, subdural);
- damage to body organs;
- poisonings – repeated (prescribed drugs, alcohol);
- failure to thrive;
- coma/unconsciousness;
- death.

There are many different forms of physical abuse, but skin, mouth and bone injuries are the most common.

Bruises

Accidental

Accidental bruises are common at places on the body where bone is fairly close to the skin. Bruises can also be found towards the front of the body, as the child usually will fall forwards.

Accidental bruises are common on the chin, nose, forehead, elbow, knees and shins. An accident-prone child can have frequent bruises in these areas. Such bruises will be diffuse, with no definite edges. Any bruising on a child before the age of mobility must be treated with concern.

Non-accidental

Bruises caused by physical abuse are more likely to occur on soft tissues, e.g. cheek, buttocks, lower back, back, thighs, calves, neck, genitalia and mouth.

Marks from slapping or grabbing may form a distinctive pattern. Slap marks might occur on buttocks/cheeks and the outlining of fingers may be seen on any part of the body. Bruises caused by direct blows with a fist have no definite pattern, but may occur in parts of the body that do not usually receive injuries by accident. A punch over the eye (black eye syndrome) or ear would be of concern. Black eyes cannot be caused by a fall on to a flat surface. Two black eyes require two injuries and must always be suspect. Other distinctive patterns of bruising may be left by the use of straps, belts, sticks and feet. The outline of the object may be left on the child in a bruise on areas such as the back or thighs (areas covered by clothing).

Bruises may be associated with shaking, which can cause serious hidden bleeding and bruising inside the skull. Any bruising around the neck is suspicious since it is very unlikely to be accidentally acquired. Other injuries may feature – ruptured eardrum/ fractured skull. Mouth injury may be a cause of concern, e.g. torn mouth (frenulum) from forced bottle-feeding.

Bone injuries

Children regularly have accidents that result in fractures. However, children's bones are more flexible than those of adults and the children themselves are lighter, so a fracture, particularly of the skull, usually signifies that considerable force has been applied.

Non-accidental

A fracture of any sort should be regarded as suspicious in a child under 8 months of age. A fracture of the skull must be regarded as particularly suspicious in a child under 3 years. Either case requires careful investigation as to the circumstances in which the fracture occurred. Swelling in the head or drowsiness may also indicate injury.

Burns

Children who have accidental burns usually have a hot liquid splashed on them by spilling or have come into contact with a hot object. The history that parents give is usually in keeping with the pattern of injury observed. However, repeated episodes may suggest inadequate care and attention to safety within the house.

Non-accidental

Children who have received non-accidental burns may exhibit a pattern that is not adequately explained by parents. The child may have been immersed in a hot liquid. The burn may show a definite line, unlike the type seen in accidental splashing. The child may also have been held against a hot object, like a radiator or a ring of a cooker, leaving distinctive marks. Cigarette burns may result in multiple small lesions in places on the skin that would not generally be exposed to danger. There may be other skin conditions that can cause similar patterns and expert paediatric advice should be sought.

Bites

Children can get bitten either by animals or humans. Animal bites (e.g. dogs) commonly puncture and tear the skin, and usually the history is definite. Small children can also bite other children.

Non-accidental

It is sometimes hard to differentiate between the bites of adults and children since measurements can be inaccurate. Any suspected adult bite mark must be taken very seriously. Consultant paediatricians may liaise with dental colleagues in order to identify marks correctly.

Poisoning

Children may commonly take medicines or chemicals that are dangerous and potentially life-threatening.

Aspects of care and safety within the home need to be considered with each event.

Non-accidental

Non-accidental poisoning can occur and may be difficult to identify, but should be suspected in bizarre or recurrent episodes and when more than one child is involved. Drowsiness or hyperventilation may be symptoms.

Shaking violently

Shaking is a frequent cause of brain damage in very young children.

Fabricated/induced illness

This occurs where parents, usually the mother (according to current research and case experience), fabricate stories of illness about their child or cause physical signs of illness. This can occur where the parent secretly administers dangerous drugs or other poisonous substances to the child, or by smothering. The symptoms that alert to the possibility of fabricated/induced illness include:

(i) symptoms that cannot be explained by any medical tests; symptoms never observed by anyone other than the parent/carer; symptoms reported to occur only at home or when a parent/carer visits a child in hospital;

(ii) high level of demand for investigation of symptoms without any documented physical sign;

(iii) unexplained problems with medical treatment, such as drips coming out or lines being interfered with; presence of unprescribed medication or poisons in the blood or urine.

5. Signs and symptoms of sexual abuse

Child sexual abuse often covers a wide spectrum of abusive activities. It rarely involves just a single incident and usually occurs over a number of years. Child sexual abuse most commonly happens within the family.

Cases of sexual abuse principally come to light through:

(a) disclosure by the child or his or her siblings/ friends;

(b) the suspicions of an adult;

(c) physical symptoms.

Colburn Faller (1989) provides a description of the wide spectrum of activities by adults which can constitute child sexual abuse. These include:

Non-contact sexual abuse

- 'Offensive sexual remarks', including statements the offender makes to the child regarding the child's sexual attributes, what he or she would like to do to the child and other sexual comments.

- Obscene phone calls.

- Independent 'exposure' involving the offender showing the victim his/her private parts and/or masturbating in front of the victim.

- 'Voyeurism' involving instances when the offender observes the victim in a state of undress or in activities that provide the offender with sexual gratification. These may include activities that others do not regard as even remotely sexually stimulating.

Sexual contact

- Involving any touching of the intimate body parts. The offender may fondle or masturbate the victim, and/or get the victim to fondle and/or masturbate them. Fondling can be either outside or inside clothes. Also includes 'frottage', i.e. where offender gains sexual gratification from rubbing his/her genitals against the victim's body or clothing.

Oral-genital sexual abuse

- Involving the offender licking, kissing, sucking or biting the child's genitals or inducing the child to do the same to them.

Interfemoral sexual abuse

- Sometimes referred to as 'dry sex' or 'vulvar intercourse', involving the offender placing his penis between the child's thighs.

Penetrative sexual abuse, of which there are four types:

- 'Digital penetration', involving putting fingers in the vagina or anus, or both. Usually the victim is penetrated by the offender, but sometimes the offender gets the child to penetrate them.
- 'Penetration with objects', involving penetration of the vagina, anus or occasionally mouth with an object.

- 'Genital penetration', involving the penis entering the vagina, sometimes partially.
- 'Anal penetration' involving the penis penetrating the anus.

Sexual exploitation

- Involves situations of sexual victimisation where the person who is responsible for the exploitation may not have direct sexual contact with the child. Two types of this abuse are child pornography and child prostitution.
- 'Child pornography' includes still photography, videos and movies, and, more recently, computer-generated pornography.
- 'Child prostitution' for the most part involves children of latency age or in adolescence. However, children as young as 4 and 5 are known to be abused in this way.

The sexual abuses described above may be found in combination with other abuses, such as physical abuse and urination and defecation on the victim. In some cases, physical abuse is an integral part of the sexual abuse; in others, drugs and alcohol may be given to the victim.

It is important to note that physical signs may not be evident in cases of sexual abuse due to the nature of the abuse and/or the fact that the disclosure was made some time after the abuse took place.

Carers and professionals should be alert to the following physical and behavioural signs:

- bleeding from the vagina/anus;

- difficulty/pain in passing urine/faeces;
- an infection may occur secondary to sexual abuse, which may or may not be a definitive sexually transmitted disease. Professionals should be informed if a child has a persistent vaginal discharge or has warts/rash in genital area;
- noticeable and uncharacteristic change of behaviour;
- hints about sexual activity;
- age-inappropriate understanding of sexual behaviour;
- inappropriate seductive behaviour;
- sexually aggressive behaviour with others;
- uncharacteristic sexual play with peers/toys;
- unusual reluctance to join in normal activities that involve undressing, e.g. games/swimming.

Particular behavioural signs and emotional problems suggestive of child abuse in young children (aged 0–10 years) include:

- mood change where the child becomes withdrawn, fearful, acting out;
- lack of concentration, especially in an educational setting;
- bed-wetting, soiling;
- pains, tummy aches, headaches with no evident physical cause;
- skin disorders;
- reluctance to go to bed, nightmares, changes in sleep patterns;
- school refusal;

- separation anxiety;
- loss of appetite, overeating, hiding food.

Particular behavioural signs and emotional problems suggestive of child abuse in older children (aged 10+ years) include:

- depression, isolation, anger;
- running away;
- drug, alcohol, solvent abuse;
- self-harm;
- suicide attempts;
- missing school or early school-leaving;
- eating disorders.

All signs/indicators need careful assessment relative to the child's circumstances.

References

Dubowitz, H. (1999), *Neglected Children: Research, Practice and Policy*. London: Sage Publications.

Skuse, D. (1989), 'Emotional Abuse and Neglect', in R. Meadow (ed.), *ABC of Child Abuse*. London: British Medical Journal Publications.

Skuse, D. and Bentovim, A. (1994), 'Physical and Emotional Maltreatment', in M. Rutter, E. Taylor and L. Hersor (eds), *Child and Adolescent Psychiatry* (3rd Edn). Oxford: Blackwell Scientific Publications.

STANDARD REPORT FORM

For reporting child protection and/or welfare concerns to the HSE.

FORM NUMBER: CC01:01:00

STANDARD REPORT FORM
(For reporting CP&W Concerns to the HSE)

Feidhmeannacht na Seirbhíse Sláinte
Health Service Executive

A. To Principal Social Worker/Designate: _____

1. Date of Report [   ]

2. Details of Child

				Male ☐	Female ☐
Name:					
Address:		DOB		Age	
		School			
Alias		Correspondence address (if different)			
Telephone		Telephone			

3. Details of Persons Reporting Concern(s)

Name:		Telephone No.	
Address:		Occupation	
		Relationship to client	

Reporter wishes to remain anonymous ☐ Reporter discussed with parents/guardians ☐

4. Parents Aware of Report

	Yes	No
Are the child's parents/carers aware that this concern is being reported to the HSE?	☐	☐

5. Details of Report

(Details of concern(s), allegation(s) or incident(s) dates, times, who was present, description of any observed injuries, parent's view(s), child's view(s) if known.)

FORM NUMBER: CC01.01:00

STANDARD REPORT FORM
(For reporting CP&W Concerns to the HSE)

Feidhmeannacht na Seirbhíse Sláinte
Health Service Executive

6. Relationships

Details of Mother		Details of Father	
Name:		Name:	
Address: (if different to child)		Address: (if different to child)	
Telephone No's:		Telephone No's:	

7. Household composition

Name	Relationship	DOB	Additional Information e.g. School/ Occupation/Other:

8. Name and Address of other personnel or agencies involved with this child

	Name	Address
Social Worker		
PHN		
GP		
Hospital		
School		
Gardaí		
Pre-School/Crèche/YG		
Other (specify):		

9. Details of person(s) allegedly causing concern in relation to the child

Relationship to child:		Age		Male ☐ Female ☐
Name:			Occupation	
Address:				

10. Details of person completing form

Name:		Occupation:	
Signed		Date:	

10.13.7.13 (12 Jul '12)

CONVENTION ON THE RIGHTS OF THE CHILD

Adopted and opened for signature, ratification and accession by General Assembly resolution 44/25 of 20 November 1989

Entry into force 2 September 1990, in accordance with article 49

Preamble

The States Parties to the present Convention,

Considering that, in accordance with the principles proclaimed in the Charter of the United Nations, recognition of the inherent dignity and of the equal and inalienable rights of all members of the human family is the foundation of freedom, justice and peace in the world,

Bearing in mind that the peoples of the United Nations have, in the Charter, reaffirmed their faith in fundamental human rights and in the dignity and worth of the human person, and have determined to promote social progress and better standards of life in larger freedom,

Recognizing that the United Nations has, in the Universal Declaration of Human Rights and in the International Covenants on Human Rights, proclaimed and agreed that everyone is entitled to all the rights and freedoms set forth therein, without distinction of any kind, such as race, colour, sex, language, religion, political or other opinion, national or social origin, property, birth or other status,

Recalling that, in the Universal Declaration of Human Rights, the United Nations has proclaimed that childhood is entitled to special care and assistance,

Convinced that the family, as the fundamental group of society and the natural environment for the growth and well-being of all its members and particularly children, should be afforded the necessary protection and assistance so that it can fully assume its responsibilities within the community,

Recognizing that the child, for the full and harmonious development of his or her personality, should grow up in a family environment, in an atmosphere of happiness, love and understanding,

Considering that the child should be fully prepared to live an individual life in society, and brought up in the spirit of the ideals proclaimed in the Charter of the United Nations, and in particular in the spirit of peace, dignity, tolerance, freedom, equality and solidarity,

Bearing in mind that the need to extend particular care to the child has been stated in the Geneva Declaration of the Rights of the Child of 1924 and in the Declaration of the Rights of the Child adopted by the General Assembly on 20 November 1959 and recognized in the Universal Declaration of Human Rights, in the International Covenant on Civil and

Political Rights (in particular in articles 23 and 24), in the International Covenant on Economic, Social and Cultural Rights (in particular in article 10) and in the statutes and relevant instruments of specialized agencies and international organizations concerned with the welfare of children,

Bearing in mind that, as indicated in the Declaration of the Rights of the Child, 'the child, by reason of his physical and mental immaturity, needs special safeguards and care, including appropriate legal protection, before as well as after birth',

Recalling the provisions of the Declaration on Social and Legal Principles relating to the Protection and Welfare of Children, with Special Reference to Foster Placement and Adoption Nationally and Internationally; the United Nations Standard Minimum Rules for the Administration of Juvenile Justice (The Beijing Rules); and the Declaration on the Protection of Women and Children in Emergency and Armed Conflict, Recognizing that, in all countries in the world, there are children living in exceptionally difficult conditions, and that such children need special consideration,

Taking due account of the importance of the traditions and cultural values of each people for the protection and harmonious development of the child, Recognizing the importance of international cooperation for improving the living conditions of children in every country, in particular in the developing countries,

Have agreed as follows:

Part I

Article 1

For the purposes of the present Convention, a child means every human being below the age of eighteen years unless under the law applicable to the child, majority is attained earlier.

Article 2

1. States Parties shall respect and ensure the rights set forth in the present Convention to each child within their jurisdiction without discrimination of any kind, irrespective of the child's or his or her parent's or legal guardian's race, colour, sex, language, religion, political or other opinion, national, ethnic or social origin, property, disability, birth or other status.

2. States Parties shall take all appropriate measures to ensure that the child is protected against all forms of discrimination or punishment on the basis of the status, activities, expressed opinions, or beliefs of the child's parents, legal guardians, or family members.

Article 3

1. In all actions concerning children, whether undertaken by public or private social welfare institutions, courts of law, administrative authorities or legislative bodies, the best interests of the child shall be a primary consideration.

2. States Parties undertake to ensure the child such protection and care as is necessary for his or her

well-being, taking into account the rights and duties of his or her parents, legal guardians, or other individuals legally responsible for him or her, and, to this end, shall take all appropriate legislative and administrative measures.

3. States Parties shall ensure that the institutions, services and facilities responsible for the care or protection of children shall conform with the standards established by competent authorities, particularly in the areas of safety, health, in the number and suitability of their staff, as well as competent supervision.

Article 4

States Parties shall undertake all appropriate legislative, administrative, and other measures for the implementation of the rights recognized in the present Convention. With regard to economic, social and cultural rights, States Parties shall undertake such measures to the maximum extent of their available resources and, where needed, within the framework of international co-operation.

Article 5

States Parties shall respect the responsibilities, rights and duties of parents or, where applicable, the members of the extended family or community as provided for by local custom, legal guardians or other persons legally responsible for the child, to provide, in a manner consistent with the evolving capacities of the child, appropriate direction and guidance in the exercise by the child of the rights recognized in the present Convention.

Article 6

1. States Parties recognize that every child has the inherent right to life.

2. States Parties shall ensure to the maximum extent possible the survival and development of the child.

Article 7

1. The child shall be registered immediately after birth and shall have the right from birth to a name, the right to acquire a nationality and, as far as possible, the right to know and be cared for by his or her parents.

2. States Parties shall ensure the implementation of these rights in accordance with their national law and their obligations under the relevant international instruments in this field, in particular where the child would otherwise be stateless.

Article 8

1. States Parties undertake to respect the right of the child to preserve his or her identity, including nationality, name and family relations as recognized by law without unlawful interference.

2. Where a child is illegally deprived of some or all of the elements of his or her identity, States Parties shall provide appropriate assistance and protection, with a view to re-establishing speedily his or her identity.

Article 9

1. States Parties shall ensure that a child shall not be separated from his or her parents against their will, except when competent authorities subject to judicial review determine, in accordance with applicable law and procedures, that such separation is necessary for the best interests of the child. Such determination may be necessary in a particular case such as one involving abuse or neglect of the child by the parents, or one where the parents are living separately and a decision must be made as to the child's place of residence.

2. In any proceedings pursuant to paragraph 1 of the present article, all interested parties shall be given an opportunity to participate in the proceedings and make their views known.

3. States Parties shall respect the right of the child who is separated from one or both parents to maintain personal relations and direct contact with both parents on a regular basis, except if it is contrary to the child's best interests.

4. Where such separation results from any action initiated by a State Party, such as the detention, imprisonment, exile, deportation or death (including death arising from any cause while the person is in the custody of the State) of one or both parents or of the child, that State Party shall, upon request, provide the parents, the child or, if appropriate, another member of the family with the essential information concerning the whereabouts of the absent member(s) of the family unless the provision of the information would be

detrimental to the well-being of the child. States Parties shall further ensure that the submission of such a request shall of itself entail no adverse consequences for the person(s) concerned.

Article 10

1. In accordance with the obligation of States Parties under article 9, paragraph 1, applications by a child or his or her parents to enter or leave a State Party for the purpose of family reunification shall be dealt with by States Parties in a positive, humane and expeditious manner. States Parties shall further ensure that the submission of such a request shall entail no adverse consequences for the applicants and for the members of their family.

2. A child whose parents reside in different States shall have the right to maintain on a regular basis, save in exceptional circumstances personal relations and direct contacts with both parents. Towards that end and in accordance with the obligation of States Parties under article 9, paragraph 1, States Parties shall respect the right of the child and his or her parents to leave any country, including their own, and to enter their own country. The right to leave any country shall be subject only to such restrictions as are prescribed by law and which are necessary to protect the national security, public order (ordre public), public health or morals or the rights and freedoms of others and are consistent with the other rights recognized in the present Convention.

Article 11

1. States Parties shall take measures to combat the illicit transfer and non-return of children abroad.

2. To this end, States Parties shall promote the conclusion of bilateral or multilateral agreements or accession to existing agreements.

Article 12

1. States Parties shall assure to the child who is capable of forming his or her own views the right to express those views freely in all matters affecting the child, the views of the child being given due weight in accordance with the age and maturity of the child.

2. For this purpose, the child shall in particular be provided the opportunity to be heard in any judicial and administrative proceedings affecting the child, either directly, or through a representative or an appropriate body, in a manner consistent with the procedural rules of national law.

Article 13

1. The child shall have the right to freedom of expression; this right shall include freedom to seek, receive and impart information and ideas of all kinds, regardless of frontiers, either orally, in writing or in print, in the form of art, or through any other media of the child's choice.

2. The exercise of this right may be subject to certain restrictions, but these shall only be such as are provided by law and are necessary:

(a) For respect of the rights or reputations of others; or

(b) For the protection of national security or of public order (ordre public), or of public health or morals.

Article 14

1. States Parties shall respect the right of the child to freedom of thought, conscience and religion.

2. States Parties shall respect the rights and duties of the parents and, when applicable, legal guardians, to provide direction to the child in the exercise of his or her right in a manner consistent with the evolving capacities of the child.

3. Freedom to manifest one's religion or beliefs may be subject only to such limitations as are prescribed by law and are necessary to protect public safety, order, health or morals, or the fundamental rights and freedoms of others.

Article 15

1. States Parties recognize the rights of the child to freedom of association and to freedom of peaceful assembly.

2. No restrictions may be placed on the exercise of these rights other than those imposed in conformity with the law and which are necessary in a democratic society in the interests of national security or public safety, public order (ordre public), the protection of public health or morals or the protection of the rights and freedoms of others.

Article 16

1. No child shall be subjected to arbitrary or unlawful interference with his or her privacy, family, home or correspondence, nor to unlawful attacks on his or her honour and reputation.

2. The child has the right to the protection of the law against such interference or attacks.

Article 17

States Parties recognize the important function performed by the mass media and shall ensure that the child has access to information and material from a diversity of national and international sources especially those aimed at the promotion of his or her social, spiritual and moral well-being and physical and mental health.

To this end, States Parties shall:

(a) Encourage the mass media to disseminate information and material of social and cultural benefit to the child and in accordance with the spirit of article 29;

(b) Encourage international co-operation in the production, exchange and dissemination of such information and material from a diversity of cultural, national and international sources;

(c) Encourage the production and dissemination of children's books;

(d) Encourage the mass media to have particular regard to the linguistic needs of the child who belongs to a minority group or who is indigenous;

(e) Encourage the development of appropriate guidelines for the protection of the child from information and material injurious to his or her well-being, bearing in mind the provisions of articles 13 and 18.

Article 18

1. States Parties shall use their best efforts to ensure recognition of the principle that both parents have common responsibilities for the upbringing and development of the child. Parents or, as the case may be, legal guardians, have the primary responsibility for the upbringing and development of the child. The best interests of the child will be their basic concern.

2. For the purpose of guaranteeing and promoting the rights set forth in the present Convention, States Parties shall render appropriate assistance to parents and legal guardians in the performance of their child-rearing responsibilities and shall ensure the development of institutions, facilities and services for the care of children.

3. States Parties shall take all appropriate measures to ensure that children of working parents have the right to benefit from child-care services and facilities for which they are eligible.

Article 19

1. States Parties shall take all appropriate legislative, administrative, social and educational measures to protect the child from all forms of physical or mental violence, injury or abuse, neglect or

negligent treatment, maltreatment or exploitation, including sexual abuse, while in the care of parent(s), legal guardian(s) or any other person who has the care of the child.

2. Such protective measures should, as appropriate, include effective procedures for the establishment of social programmes to provide necessary support for the child and for those who have the care of the child, as well as for other forms of prevention and for identification, reporting, referral, investigation, treatment and follow-up of instances of child maltreatment described heretofore, and, as appropriate, for judicial involvement.

Article 20

1. A child temporarily or permanently deprived of his or her family environment, or in whose own best interests cannot be allowed to remain in that environment, shall be entitled to special protection and assistance provided by the State.

2. States Parties shall in accordance with their national laws ensure alternative care for such a child.

3. Such care could include, inter alia, foster placement, kafalah of Islamic law, adoption or if necessary placement in suitable institutions for the care of children. When considering solutions, due regard shall be paid to the desirability of continuity in a child's upbringing and to the child's ethnic, religious, cultural and linguistic background.

Article 21

States Parties that recognize and/or permit the system of adoption shall ensure that the best interests of the child shall be the paramount consideration and they shall:

(a) Ensure that the adoption of a child is authorized only by competent authorities who determine, in accordance with applicable law and procedures and on the basis of all pertinent and reliable information, that the adoption is permissible in view of the child's status concerning parents, relatives and legal guardians and that, if required, the persons concerned have given their informed consent to the adoption on the basis of such counselling as may be necessary;

(b) Recognize that inter-country adoption may be considered as an alternative means of child's care, if the child cannot be placed in a foster or an adoptive family or cannot in any suitable manner be cared for in the child's country of origin;

(c) Ensure that the child concerned by inter-country adoption enjoys safeguards and standards equivalent to those existing in the case of national adoption;

(d) Take all appropriate measures to ensure that, in inter-country adoption, the placement does not result in improper financial gain for those involved in it;

(e) Promote, where appropriate, the objectives of the present article by concluding bilateral or multilateral arrangements or agreements, and endeavour, within this framework, to ensure that the placement of the child in another country is carried out by competent authorities or organs.

Article 22

1. States Parties shall take appropriate measures to ensure that a child who is seeking refugee status or who is considered a refugee in accordance with applicable international or domestic law and procedures shall, whether unaccompanied or accompanied by his or her parents or by any other person, receive appropriate protection and humanitarian assistance in the enjoyment of applicable rights set forth in the present Convention and in other international human rights or humanitarian instruments to which the said States are Parties.

2. For this purpose, States Parties shall provide, as they consider appropriate, co-operation in any efforts by the United Nations and other competent intergovernmental organizations or nongovern-mental organizations co-operating with the United Nations to protect and assist such a child and to trace the parents or other members of the family of any refugee child in order to obtain information necessary for reunification with his or her family. In cases where no parents or other members of the family can be found, the child shall be accorded the same protection as any other child permanently or temporarily deprived of his or her family environment for any reason, as set forth in the present Convention.

Article 23

1. States Parties recognize that a mentally or physically disabled child should enjoy a full and decent life, in conditions which ensure dignity, promote self-reliance and facilitate the child's active participation in the community.

2. States Parties recognize the right of the disabled child to special care and shall encourage and ensure the extension, subject to available resources, to the eligible child and those responsible for his or her care, of assistance for which application is made and which is appropriate to the child's condition and to the circumstances of the parents or others caring for the child.

3. Recognizing the special needs of a disabled child, assistance extended in accordance with paragraph 2 of the present article shall be provided free of charge, whenever possible, taking into account the financial resources of the parents or others caring for the child, and shall be designed to ensure that the disabled child has effective access to and receives education, training, health care services, rehabilitation services, preparation for employment and recreation opportunities in a manner conducive to the child's achieving the fullest possible social integration and individual development, including his or her cultural and spiritual development.

4. States Parties shall promote, in the spirit of inter-national cooperation, the exchange of appropriate information in the field of preventive health care

and of medical, psychological and functional treatment of disabled children, including dissemination of and access to information concerning methods of rehabilitation, education and vocational services, with the aim of enabling States Parties to improve their capabilities and skills and to widen their experience in these areas. In this regard, particular account shall be taken of the needs of developing countries.

Article 24

1. States Parties recognize the right of the child to the enjoyment of the highest attainable standard of health and to facilities for the treatment of illness and rehabilitation of health. States Parties shall strive to ensure that no child is deprived of his or her right of access to such health care services.

2. States Parties shall pursue full implementation of this right and, in particular, shall take appropriate measures:

    (a) To diminish infant and child mortality;

    (b) To ensure the provision of necessary medical assistance and health care to all children with emphasis on the development of primary health care;

    (c) To combat disease and malnutrition, including within the framework of primary health care, through, inter alia, the application of readily available technology and through the provision of adequate nutritious foods and clean drinking-water, taking into consideration the dangers and risks of environmental pollution;

(d) To ensure appropriate pre-natal and post-natal health care for mothers;

(e) To ensure that all segments of society, in particular parents and children, are informed, have access to education and are supported in the use of basic knowledge of child health and nutrition, the advantages of breastfeeding, hygiene and environmental sanitation and the prevention of accidents;

(f) To develop preventive health care, guidance for parents and family planning education and services.

3. States Parties shall take all effective and appropriate measures with a view to abolishing traditional practices prejudicial to the health of children.

4. States Parties undertake to promote and encourage international co-operation with a view to achieving progressively the full realization of the right recognized in the present article. In this regard, particular account shall be taken of the needs of developing countries.

Article 25

States Parties recognize the right of a child who has been placed by the competent authorities for the purposes of care, protection or treatment of his or her physical or mental health, to a periodic review of the treatment provided to the child and all other circumstances relevant to his or her placement.

Article 26

1. States Parties shall recognize for every child the right to benefit from social security, including social insurance, and shall take the necessary measures to achieve the full realization of this right in accordance with their national law.

2. The benefits should, where appropriate, be granted, taking into account the resources and the circumstances of the child and persons having responsibility for the maintenance of the child, as well as any other consideration relevant to an application for benefits made by or on behalf of the child.

Article 27

1. States Parties recognize the right of every child to a standard of living adequate for the child's physical, mental, spiritual, moral and social development.

2. The parent(s) or others responsible for the child have the primary responsibility to secure, within their abilities and financial capacities, the conditions of living necessary for the child's development.

3. States Parties, in accordance with national conditions and within their means, shall take appropriate measures to assist parents and others responsible for the child to implement this right and shall in case of need provide material assistance and support programmes, particularly with regard to nutrition, clothing and housing.

4. States Parties shall take all appropriate measures to secure the recovery of maintenance for the child from the parents or other persons having financial responsibility for the child, both within the State Party and from abroad. In particular, where the person having financial responsibility for the child lives in a State different from that of the child, States Parties shall promote the accession to international agreements or the conclusion of such agreements, as well as the making of other appropriate arrangements.

Article 28

1. States Parties recognize the right of the child to education, and with a view to achieving this right progressively and on the basis of equal opportunity, they shall, in particular:

    (a) Make primary education compulsory and available free to all;

    (b) Encourage the development of different forms of secondary education, including general and vocational education, make them available and accessible to every child, and take appropriate measures such as the introduction of free education and offering financial assistance in case of need;

    (c) Make higher education accessible to all on the basis of capacity by every appropriate means;

    (d) Make educational and vocational information and guidance available and accessible to all children;

(e) Take measures to encourage regular attendance at schools and the reduction of drop-out rates.

2. States Parties shall take all appropriate measures to ensure that school discipline is administered in a manner consistent with the child's human dignity and in conformity with the present Convention.

3. States Parties shall promote and encourage international cooperation in matters relating to education, in particular with a view to contributing to the elimination of ignorance and illiteracy throughout the world and facilitating access to scientific and technical knowledge and modern teaching methods. In this regard, particular account shall be taken of the needs of developing countries.

Article 29

1. States Parties agree that the education of the child shall be directed to:

   (a) The development of the child's personality, talents and mental and physical abilities to their fullest potential;

   (b) The development of respect for human rights and fundamental freedoms, and for the principles enshrined in the Charter of the United Nations;

   (c) The development of respect for the child's parents, his or her own cultural identity, language and values, for the national values of the country in which the child is living, the country from which he or she may originate, and for civilizations different from his or her own;

(d) The preparation of the child for responsible life in a free society, in the spirit of understanding, peace, tolerance, equality of sexes, and friendship among all peoples, ethnic, national and religious groups and persons of indigenous origin;

(e) The development of respect for the natural environment.

2. No part of the present article or article 28 shall be construed so as to interfere with the liberty of individuals and bodies to establish and direct educational institutions, subject always to the observance of the principle set forth in paragraph 1 of the present article and to the requirements that the education given in such institutions shall conform to such minimum standards as may be laid down by the State.

Article 30

In those States in which ethnic, religious or linguistic minorities or persons of indigenous origin exist, a child belonging to such a minority or who is indigenous shall not be denied the right, in community with other members of his or her group, to enjoy his or her own culture, to profess and practise his or her own religion, or to use his or her own language.

Article 31

1. States Parties recognize the right of the child to rest and leisure, to engage in play and recreational activities appropriate to the age of the child and to participate freely in cultural life and the arts.

2. States Parties shall respect and promote the right of the child to participate fully in cultural and artistic life and shall encourage the provision of appropriate and equal opportunities for cultural, artistic, recreational and leisure activity.

Article 32

1. States Parties recognize the right of the child to be protected from economic exploitation and from performing any work that is likely to be hazardous or to interfere with the child's education, or to be harmful to the child's health or physical, mental, spiritual, moral or social development.

2. States Parties shall take legislative, administrative, social and educational measures to ensure the implementation of the present article. To this end, and having regard to the relevant provisions of other international instruments, States Parties shall in particular:

   (a) Provide for a minimum age or minimum ages for admission to employment;

   (b) Provide for appropriate regulation of the hours and conditions of employment;

   (c) Provide for appropriate penalties or other sanctions to ensure the effective enforcement of the present article.

Article 33

States Parties shall take all appropriate measures, including legislative, administrative, social and educational measures, to protect children from the illicit use of narcotic drugs and psychotropic substances as defined in the relevant international treaties, and to prevent the use of children in the illicit production and trafficking of such substances.

Article 34

States Parties undertake to protect the child from all forms of sexual exploitation and sexual abuse. For these purposes, States Parties shall in particular take all appropriate national, bilateral and multilateral measures to prevent:

(a) The inducement or coercion of a child to engage in any unlawful sexual activity;

(b) The exploitative use of children in prostitution or other unlawful sexual practices;

(c) The exploitative use of children in pornographic performances and materials.

Article 35

States Parties shall take all appropriate national, bilateral and multilateral measures to prevent the abduction of, the sale of or traffic in children for any purpose or in any form.

Article 36

States Parties shall protect the child against all other forms of exploitation prejudicial to any aspects of the child's welfare.

Article 37

States Parties shall ensure that:

(a)   No child shall be subjected to torture or other cruel, inhuman or degrading treatment or punishment. Neither capital punishment nor life imprisonment without possibility of release shall be imposed for offences committed by persons below eighteen years of age;

(b)   No child shall be deprived of his or her liberty unlawfully or arbitrarily. The arrest, detention or imprisonment of a child shall be in conformity with the law and shall be used only as a measure of last resort and for the shortest appropriate period of time;

(c)   Every child deprived of liberty shall be treated with humanity and respect for the inherent dignity of the human person, and in a manner which takes into account the needs of persons of his or her age. In particular, every child deprived of liberty shall be separated from adults unless it is considered in the child's best interest not to do so and shall have the right to maintain contact with his or her family through correspondence and visits, save in exceptional circumstances;

(d)   Every child deprived of his or her liberty shall have the right to prompt access to legal and other appropriate assistance, as well as the right to challenge the legality of the deprivation of his or her liberty before a court or other competent, independent and impartial authority, and to a prompt decision on any such action.

Article 38

1. States Parties undertake to respect and to ensure respect for rules of international humanitarian law applicable to them in armed conflicts which are relevant to the child.

2. States Parties shall take all feasible measures to ensure that persons who have not attained the age of fifteen years do not take a direct part in hostilities.

3. States Parties shall refrain from recruiting any person who has not attained the age of fifteen years into their armed forces. In recruiting among those persons who have attained the age of fifteen years but who have not attained the age of eighteen years, States Parties shall endeavour to give priority to those who are oldest.

4. In accordance with their obligations under international humanitarian law to protect the civilian population in armed conflicts, States Parties shall take all feasible measures to ensure protection and care of children who are affected by an armed conflict.

Article 39

States Parties shall take all appropriate measures to promote physical and psychological recovery and social reintegration of a child victim of: any form of neglect, exploitation, or abuse; torture or any other form of cruel, inhuman or degrading treatment or punishment; or armed conflicts. Such recovery and reintegration shall take place in an environment which fosters the health, self-respect and dignity of the child.

Article 40

1. States Parties recognize the right of every child alleged as, accused of, or recognized as having infringed the penal law to be treated in a manner consistent with the promotion of the child's sense of dignity and worth, which reinforces the child's respect for the human rights and fundamental freedoms of others and which takes into account the child's age and the desirability of promoting the child's reintegration and the child's assuming a constructive role in society.

2. To this end, and having regard to the relevant provisions of international instruments, States Parties shall, in particular, ensure that:

   (a) No child shall be alleged as, be accused of, or recognized as having infringed the penal law by reason of acts or omissions that were not prohibited by national or international law at the time they were committed;

   (b) Every child alleged as or accused of having infringed the penal law has at least the following guarantees:

      (i) To be presumed innocent until proven guilty according to law;

      (ii) To be informed promptly and directly of the charges against him or her, and, if appropriate, through his or her parents or legal guardians, and to have legal or other appropriate assistance in the preparation and presentation of his or her defence;

(iii) To have the matter determined without delay by a competent, independent and impartial authority or judicial body in a fair hearing according to law, in the presence of legal or other appropriate assistance and, unless it is considered not to be in the best interest of the child, in particular, taking into account his or her age or situation, his or her parents or legal guardians;

(iv) Not to be compelled to give testimony or to confess guilt; to examine or have examined adverse witnesses and to obtain the participation and examination of witnesses on his or her behalf under conditions of equality;

(v) If considered to have infringed the penal law, to have this decision and any measures imposed in consequence thereof reviewed by a higher competent, independent and impartial authority or judicial body according to law;

(vi) To have the free assistance of an interpreter if the child cannot understand or speak the language used;

(vii) To have his or her privacy fully respected at all stages of the proceedings.

3. States Parties shall seek to promote the establishment of laws, procedures, authorities and institutions specifically applicable to children alleged as, accused of, or recognized as having infringed the penal law, and, in particular:

(a) The establishment of a minimum age below which children shall be presumed not to have the capacity to infringe the penal law;

(b) Whenever appropriate and desirable, measures for dealing with such children without resorting to judicial proceedings, providing that human rights and legal safeguards are fully respected.

4. A variety of dispositions, such as care, guidance and supervision orders; counselling; probation; foster care; education and vocational training programmes and other alternatives to institutional care shall be available to ensure that children are dealt with in a manner appropriate to their well-being and proportionate both to their circumstances and the offence.

Article 41

Nothing in the present Convention shall affect any provisions which are more conducive to the realization of the rights of the child and which may be contained in:

(a) The law of a State party; or

(b) International law in force for that State.

Part II

Article 42

States Parties undertake to make the principles and provisions of the Convention widely known, by appropriate and active means, to adults and children alike.

Article 43

1. For the purpose of examining the progress made by States Parties in achieving the realization of the obligations undertaken in the present Convention, there shall be established a Committee on the Rights of the Child, which shall carry out the functions hereinafter provided.

2. The Committee shall consist of eighteen experts of high moral standing and recognized competence in the field covered by this Convention. The members of the Committee shall be elected by States Parties from among their nationals and shall serve in their personal capacity, consideration being given to equitable geographical distribution, as well as to the principal legal systems.

3. The members of the Committee shall be elected by secret ballot from a list of persons nominated by States Parties. Each State Party may nominate one person from among its own nationals.

4. The initial election to the Committee shall be held no later than six months after the date of the entry into force of the present Convention and thereafter every second year. At least four months before the date of each election, the Secretary-General of the United Nations shall address a letter to States Parties inviting them to submit their nominations within two months. The Secretary-General shall subsequently prepare a list in alphabetical order of all persons thus nominated, indicating States Parties which have nominated them, and shall submit it to the States Parties to the present Convention.

5. The elections shall be held at meetings of States Parties convened by the Secretary-General at United Nations Headquarters. At those meetings, for which two thirds of States Parties shall constitute a quorum, the persons elected to the Committee shall be those who obtain the largest number of votes and an absolute majority of the votes of the representatives of States Parties present and voting.

6. The members of the Committee shall be elected for a term of four years. They shall be eligible for re-election if renominated. The term of five of the members elected at the first election shall expire at the end of two years; immediately after the first election, the names of these five members shall be chosen by lot by the Chairman of the meeting.

7. If a member of the Committee dies or resigns or declares that for any other cause he or she can no longer perform the duties of the Committee, the State Party which nominated the member shall appoint another expert from among its nationals to serve for the remainder of the term, subject to the approval of the Committee.

8. The Committee shall establish its own rules of procedure.

9. The Committee shall elect its officers for a period of two years.

10. The meetings of the Committee shall normally be held at United Nations Headquarters or at any other convenient place as determined by the Committee. The Committee shall normally meet

annually. The duration of the meetings of the Committee shall be determined, and reviewed, if necessary, by a meeting of the States Parties to the present Convention, subject to the approval of the General Assembly.

11. The Secretary-General of the United Nations shall provide the necessary staff and facilities for the effective performance of the functions of the Committee under the present Convention.

12. With the approval of the General Assembly, the members of the Committee established under the present Convention shall receive emoluments from United Nations resources on such terms and conditions as the Assembly may decide.

Article 44

1. States Parties undertake to submit to the Committee, through the Secretary-General of the United Nations, reports on the measures they have adopted which give effect to the rights recognized herein and on the progress made on the enjoyment of those rights

    (a) Within two years of the entry into force of the Convention for the State Party concerned;

    (b) Thereafter every five years.

2. Reports made under the present article shall indicate factors and difficulties, if any, affecting the degree of fulfilment of the obligations under the present Convention. Reports shall also contain sufficient information to provide the Committee with a comprehensive understanding of the

implementation of the Convention in the country concerned.

3. A State Party which has submitted a comprehensive initial report to the Committee need not, in its subsequent reports submitted in accordance with paragraph 1 (b) of the present article, repeat basic information previously provided.

4. The Committee may request from States Parties further information relevant to the implementation of the Convention.

5. The Committee shall submit to the General Assembly, through the Economic and Social Council, every two years, reports on its activities.

6. States Parties shall make their reports widely available to the public in their own countries.

Article 45

In order to foster the effective implementation of the Convention and to encourage international cooperation in the field covered by the Convention:

(a) The specialized agencies, the United Nations Children's Fund, and other United Nations organs shall be entitled to be represented at the consideration of the implementation of such provisions of the present Convention as fall within the scope of their mandate. The Committee may invite the specialized agencies, the United Nations Children's Fund and other competent bodies as it may consider appropriate to provide expert advice on the implementation of the Convention in areas falling within the scope of their respective mandates. The Committee may invite the specialized agencies, the United Nations Children's Fund, and other United Nations organs to submit reports on the implementation of the Convention in areas falling within the scope of their activities;

(b) The Committee shall transmit, as it may consider appropriate, to the specialized agencies, the United Nations Children's Fund and other competent bodies, any reports from States Parties that contain a request, or indicate a need, for technical advice or assistance, along with the Committee's observations and suggestions, if any, on these requests or indications;

(c) The Committee may recommend to the General Assembly to request the Secretary-General to undertake on its behalf studies on specific issues relating to the rights of the child;

(d) The Committee may make suggestions and general recommendations based on information received pursuant to articles 44 and 45 of the present Convention. Such suggestions and general recommendations shall be transmitted to any State Party concerned and reported to the General Assembly, together with comments, if any, from States Parties.

Part III

Article 46

The present Convention shall be open for signature by all States.

Article 47

The present Convention is subject to ratification. Instruments of ratification shall be deposited with the Secretary-General of the United Nations.

Article 48

The present Convention shall remain open for accession by any State. The instruments of accession shall be deposited with the Secretary-General of the United Nations.

Article 49

1. The present Convention shall enter into force on the thirtieth day following the date of deposit with the Secretary-General of the United Nations of the twentieth instrument of ratification or accession.

2. For each State ratifying or acceding to the Convention after the deposit of the twentieth instrument of ratification or accession, the Convention shall enter into force on the thirtieth day after the deposit by such State of its instrument of ratification or accession.

Article 50

1. Any State Party may propose an amendment and file it with the Secretary-General of the United Nations. The Secretary-General shall thereupon communicate the proposed amendment to States Parties, with a request that they indicate whether they favour a conference of States Parties for the purpose of considering and voting upon the proposals. In the event that, within four months

from the date of such communication, at least one third of the States Parties favour such a conference, the Secretary-General shall convene the conference under the auspices of the United Nations. Any amendment adopted by a majority of States Parties present and voting at the conference shall be submitted to the General Assembly for approval.

2. An amendment adopted in accordance with paragraph 1 of the present article shall enter into force when it has been approved by the General Assembly of the United Nations and accepted by a two-thirds majority of States Parties.

3. When an amendment enters into force, it shall be binding on those States Parties which have accepted it, other States Parties still being bound by the provisions of the present Convention and any earlier amendments which they have accepted.

Article 51

1. The Secretary-General of the United Nations shall receive and circulate to all States the text of reservations made by States at the time of ratification or accession.

2. A reservation incompatible with the object and purpose of the present Convention shall not be permitted.

3. Reservations may be withdrawn at any time by notification to that effect addressed to the Secretary-General of the United Nations, who shall then inform all States. Such notification shall

take effect on the date on which it is received by the Secretary-General.

Article 52

A State Party may denounce the present Convention by written notification to the Secretary-General of the United Nations. Denunciation becomes effective one year after the date of receipt of the notification by the Secretary-General.

Article 53

The Secretary-General of the United Nations is designated as the depositary of the present Convention.

Article 54

The original of the present Convention, of which the Arabic, Chinese, English, French, Russian and Spanish texts are equally authentic, shall be deposited with the Secretary-General of the United Nations. IN WITNESS THEREOF the undersigned plenipotentiaries, being duly authorized thereto by their respective governments, have signed the present Convention.

GLOSSARY

A mensa et thoro A Latin phrase that literally translates as 'from board and bed'. When used in a divorce context it means that the couple do not live together. This expression is an old one and the equivalent in modern terminology is 'being separated'.

Anomaly Something that is different from what is expected.

Antecedent rights Rights that are already in existence.

Article A clause in an agreement or document.

Capacity The ability or power to do something or a person's legal competence.

Care contract The level of trust that is involved in a caring position such as childcare or teaching. It entails a commitment to providing care in place of someone else or indeed along with somebody else where everybody has a role in the care that is provided.

Common good   This expression is found throughout the Irish Constitution and means that some individual rights are limited so as not to interfere unnecessarily with other people's needs and rights. In other words, a balance is required and this may restrict the application of some of our rights so that we can all live together equally as a society.

Constitution   Most countries have a written constitution that sets out the rules and procedures by which that country and individuals in that country are governed and the method by which its laws are drawn up.

Contemporaneous   Contemporaneous notes are those made at that moment in time, i.e. they are made at the moment that the action you are recording is taking place. They would usually be dated and therefore in a diary they are made as you go along rather than say a week later.

Convention   A written agreement, usually of an international nature, which is adopted by states to govern

	whatever is covered by the convention.
Guardian *ad litem*	Somebody appointed to look after the best interests of the child and to read and inform themselves with the facts on behalf of the child and to give an objective opinion to the judge on what would best serve the best interests of that child.
Imprescriptible rights	Rights that exist whether you use them or not – they cannot be ignored.
In loco parentis	A person acting in place of parents on behalf of a child or dependent person.
Inalienable rights	Rights that cannot be removed, transferred or altered.
Latency age	The stage between being a child and being an adolescent; in other words, it refers to a child who is in the process of developing or approaching puberty.
Laws	The rules that are written down as Acts of government, such as the Child Care Act 1991.

Legally binding Something that has legal protection and cannot be changed without getting court approval.

Legislation All or part of a country's written law. Usually in Ireland this relates to Acts of government, an example of which would be the Child Care Act 1991.

Preamble An introductory statement that usually explains the intentions of what is to be presented.

Protocol The accepted code of behaviour or action in relation to a certain thing or situation that might arise.

Protracted Long-drawn-out process or requiring much discussion.

Ratified Where an agreement, treaty, convention or some other agreement is signed as having effect.

Referendum The name given to the voting process that is used in relation to proposed changes to the Constitution. The Irish Constitution states that a person who is registered to vote essentially has the right to vote in a referendum.

Repatriation

Sending somebody back to their country of origin.

States party

In this book this term refers to the countries who signed up to the UN Convention on the Rights of the Child (as an example). When a state agrees to accept the ideals of the Convention it is known as a state party – in other words, the state is a party to the agreement (as in having to do something).

INDEX